To Nelson –

Best of life and
to you and yours –

John Stachura

5-15-2010

The Mind

User Manual

Release 1.0

By John P. Stachura

Bloomington, IN Milton Keynes, UK
authorHOUSE®

AuthorHouse™
1663 Liberty Drive, Suite 200
Bloomington, IN 47403
www.authorhouse.com
Phone: 1-800-839-8640

AuthorHouse™ UK Ltd.
500 Avebury Boulevard
Central Milton Keynes, MK9 2BE
www.authorhouse.co.uk
Phone: 08001974150

First published by AuthorHouse 4/4/2007

ISBN: 978-1-4343-0512-1 (e)
ISBN: 978-1-4343-0511-4 (sc)

Library of Congress Control Number: 2007902365

Printed in the United States of America
Bloomington, Indiana

This book is printed on acid-free paper.

Amazing Gracie

The one I love is Grace by name
She shows her love and has no shame
She shows she cares and spends her love
Like rays of sunshine from above

I run from her only to find
That she is always in my mind
It's difficult to understand
Why she chose me to make life grand

When she feels hurt, I cannot live
To ease her pain, I have to give
I fall behind, but not for long
Because our love is true and strong

I look forward to greet each day
With Grace by me so we can play
It's Here and Now for endless time
There's no limit for Love Sublime

So, together, we create life
Loving husband and loving wife
One time I thought I had no place
But I found it - Amazing Grace.

Table of Contents

Introduction

*"The simple secret of the universe is
that you create your own reality."*

Captain Edgar D. Mitchell, Apollo 14 astronaut

This book will be a work in progress. Participation in improving its message and content will be welcomed on the Internet. The Ebook will be dynamic and occasionally create a new release in paper form. It should get better with more and more contributions.

On February 8, 1982, I found my mind. I hadn't even known I had lost it. I really hadn't lost it, but I had more or less not paid any attention to it for a long time. I guess I had placed it on automatic pilot and found myself somewhere I did not want to be. This was a day that cannot be forgotten because it was one of those experiences that come once in a lifetime. Call it epiphany, enlightenment, flash of insight, whatever. I certainly could never look at life as I had before. All the experiences I had from my birth until this awakening came together and meshed into one holistic vision that connected all the knowledge I had gathered during my life.

This experience set me off on a quest for understanding. What is this thing called mind? Why is it that some people see things one way and others see it differently? Is there not only one real view? Why do we take different "Points of View" and choose to argue about what we see? For example, if we are on the rim of the Grand Canyon, observing the grandeur and color of its magnificence, we could communicate about what we see and enhance each other's "point of view" and come away with a better view. Those other people we waved to across the gap have a different point of view. It would be interesting to know how they viewed the canyon. Regardless of whose view(s) we prefer, does that change what the canyon is?

I started programming computers for LaSalle National Bank in 1963, the day after John Kennedy was murdered. Programming was an infant profession then. Everyone was new at it and there was very little standardization for anyone to follow. Each programmer used whatever method conceivable (personal points of view) to accomplish tasks. I started at the era of Hollerith code cards. These cards contained 80 columns and were the only storage medium used at the bank, at first. Each column had numbers from 0 through 9 and two additional "zones" above the numbers. This allowed for twenty-seven possible combinations that would cover the twenty-six letters of the alphabet and a "/." The Central Processing Unit (CPU) held all of 8 kilobytes! The nice thing about such a simplistic system was that a core memory dump was not very large and patches to correct errors could be entered in machine language if a program failed. This was similar to the Wild West development but in an electronic country. Every new program was an adventure.

Sometime after creating individual programs, we began looking at programs within processes as *systems*. Systems analyst became a title to be coveted. A "system" is defined as an ordered whole comprised of related parts. All systems are identical in the way they work and all must be connected to exist. The only difference from one system to another is what they use for input to create their output. There are no independent systems. This idea is one key that created my epiphany. We also are "systems," so we must be connected to all other systems.

After reading hundreds of books and gaining more years of experience in the computer industry, it started becoming clear that computer usage was beginning to mirror the human mind. From the time I started programming, we went from Hollerith code punched cards to tape, to disk, to today's media. Methods went from data processing to information processing to knowledge processing to today's intelligent systems. Huge advances were being made, but, along with those advances, systems became more cumbersome and harder to maintain. We were wallowing in complexity and could not extricate ourselves. Rube Goldberg would be proud of some of those designs.

I met Paul Tedesco in 1991. Paul had begun programming a year after I had started, after he received a master's degree in Mathematics. He and I schmoozed at some common functions in Chicago and started talking about working together. He had created software he called "Slice and Dice" and used it in consulting assignments when he worked for companies that hired his services. I had been involved for years in marketing software for large software firms and was accustomed to making presentations to large Information Technology (IT) groups and upper management of Fortune 500 companies. Paul wanted to find a "rainmaker" to help him market his invention. In August 1994, he asked me to accompany him to Purdue University. He was giving a presentation for the purpose of selling his services and wanted me to give him a critique of how he came across. I agreed.

When Paul began his presentation, it was relatively common in content and much verbiage was "boilerplate" for the business. Soon, however, he began describing how his software tool "Slice and Dice" worked and I started paying close attention to what he was saying. By the time he was finished, I had a very good idea of the potential of what he had created. As we were heading back to Chicago, we talked more of the details in his software and, by the time we reached his home, it was clear to me what we had. I said to him: "Paul, you have designed the core of an Artificial Mind!" At first, he did not know what I meant, so we began discussing our thoughts.

Slice and Dice reversed the way programs are written. Virtually all application software is written to process known transactions in a specific sequence to fulfill their requirements. This is done first by defining transaction codes in a program that it will encounter when reading a file. The program recognizes each input transaction code based upon the definitions given and will update appropriate files based on the content. This input may be from any variety of peripheral equipment, but today, the point of Sale (POS) transaction usually begins a company's processes. Varieties of this method are endless, but most programs will follow these basic steps. Large companies have millions of lines of code to serve their myriad transactions in this fashion.

Paul's software creates programs dynamically from a store of reusable code and its associated knowledge base. It is the transaction itself that makes Cogitator create whatever software instructions necessary to satisfy it. This is exactly how you address your daily tasks. Each item on your "To Do List" is a transaction for you to accomplish with your knowledge base. The circumstances for each activity determine what instructions you will process through your neural networks. If conditions change, you can adapt and fire off a different sequence of instructions to compensate. Slice/Dice can do the same.

What this means is program maintenance is no longer necessary. Virtually all programming code can be contained on a small piece of storage. There are really very few instructions in programming languages. With Paul's software, all that need be done when changes occur in the structure is to change lists of definitions and/or relationships.

Paul had been studying Artificial Intelligence for many years (as had I) and was a member of many groups who were in the same milieu. I had read "The Cognitive Computer" by Roger Schenk some time prior to meeting Paul and knew Roger was on the wrong track. For some reason, though, Paul had found the way to make the computer operate the same way we do. We named the product "Cogitator" and founded Cognitor, Inc. This was just the beginning, however.

Cognitor was the name I was given after going through a Rosicrucian ritual. (Information is at www.amorc.com and www.rosicrucian-order.com.) It was chosen from a group of potential secret names for new initiates. I had been studying "The Mastery of Life" for three years and reached a point of study where I could actually have a name in the society. The name is defined in the Oxford English Dictionary (OED) as "an advocate or procurator." In other words, one who speaks on behalf of someone against an adversary. I liked the name enough to give it to the company Paul and I founded eight years later.

Although Paul and I had no trouble conversing about how the human mind works and how we can replicate it in a machine, it turns out there are a lot of people who have absolutely no idea how their mind works. In presenting this product and our company, we found that most of our audience could not grasp what could be done with an Artificial Mind. Over the next couple of years, frustration became unbearable. I had to step away and let others carry the ball. I had gone broke trying to get this idea going and had to get gainful employment. I continued researching for more years until I could actually get a clear picture of what to say and this book is the result.

As of this writing, Cognitor, Inc. is primarily occupied with Customer Relationship Management (CRM), but this is only the beginning. It has greatly improved the response time (and accuracy of such response) to customer service calls and the needed processing to solve problems. The product *learns* from skilled technicians as the problems are solved and, once solved, need not ask for the same solution again. This reduces the time and effort of each call and, eventually, will allow first-call solution in over ninety percent of cases. A HUGE saving. Recently, major upgrades have been made to give Cogitator increased potential.

There is no question that this concept is the end-all for computerization if it is carried to its eventual potential. There is nothing the human ego can think that cannot be downloaded into Cogitator. The things I learned in the process of creating Cogitator though, forced me to understand how my mind actually works. It has been an excruciating process to finally understand what this mind can do. Instead of complicating my life, it has distilled it to a very simple and rewarding understanding of life - it all eventually boils down to a zero and a one.

"When you are inspired by some great purpose, some extraordinary project, all your thoughts break their bonds. Your mind transcends limitations, your consciousness expands in every direction and you find yourself in a new, great, and wonderful world. Dormant forces, faculties and talents become alive and you discover yourself to be a greater person by far than you ever dreamed yourself to be."

- Patanjali

The Operating System

*"We do not receive wisdom, we must discover it for
ourselves, after a journey through the wilderness
which no one else can make for us, which no one
can spare us, for our wisdom is the point of view
from which we come at last to regard the world."*

Marcel Proust

Having a mind is being aware, or awake. Any computer you buy today will include an Operating System. This is necessary to make the computer "aware" of what kind of peripheral equipment it will use to communicate with you. You also were born with an "Operating System." Yours knows how many times per minute to beat your heart, what temperature your body should maintain, how to exchange carbon dioxide for oxygen, how to digest food, purge poison, etc. You know a lot more than you think. Soon after you were born though, you started burying your Operating System with "applications" in the same way programmers create applications for the computer's operating system to execute.

The human operating system has only one purpose in its mind – to keep the body that contains it in **Balance**. It exists only to keep you healthy. It doesn't know to do anything else. It is the same system that operates in all life. An acorn contains the operating system to become a balanced oak tree; a nautilus has the operating system that keeps it building chambers to stay in balance; a condor egg contains the operating system that allows it to soar the thermals as a balanced adult bird. All life uses the very same operating system to be what it is. The difference among life forms is the instructions contained in their operating systems. Everything that is became what it is because it is in balance. The operating system for any organism is contained in the double helix of its DNA.

3

There is one more element of mind that must be understood. For any organism to develop into a greater being, it must execute its instructions in **Sequence**. Two laws of life that cannot be violated are Balance and Sequence. Balance is the desired State of Being for every being and sequence is the only way to execute a Process of coming to be (becoming) a different State of Being. If you do not execute a process in an ordered sequence, you will have to suffer the **con**-sequences. All that means is that you took a detour and have to return to the last correct action.

Your operating system is made up of two elements: genes and memes. Memes contain your character traits passed from generation to generation. Genes build your physical characteristics and memes build your mind's character. This is what creates the concept of body/soul. These two elements are interdependent, just like Einstein's time/space continuum. One cannot exist without the other. In Cogitator, this concept is replicated with the 0/1 of binary.

Problems arise when a human being wants to create a "mind of his own." It is no mystery to Paul and me that Cogitator is the same as a human ego. However, it doesn't have the one element that makes people do stupid things. It doesn't have emotion. All it can do is think and learn. It cannot feel. Virtually all human decisions are motivated by emotion and this trait is actually how people are controlled in society. The reason

Cogitator doesn't have emotion is that it doesn't have a body. The human body has "feelings." Not so with Cogitator. It is pure logic. The only sense it contains is Common Sense.

If you let your operating system run your life, you will suffer few con-sequences. If you let your feelings (ego) get control, you definitely will suffer. Before we go too far with this comparison, we need to know how we are able to achieve anything with any mind. Now that we know there are only two concerns for any mind to consider, (balance and sequence) how can we get to know what prevents us from being whatever we want to be?

If you are alive and aware of life, what else do you need? When you were born, you became aware of your mom's touch, her warm flesh and comforting strokes, the smell of her bosom, as well as her cooing words. Soon, your eyes focused on her face and she became indelibly etched in your memory. When you became hungry or soiled (out of balance) your cries would bring her to put you back in balance. As you developed, you found your toes, your father's mustache, your uncle's glasses and other fascinating objects to explore. Each experience was a brick in the foundation of your knowledge base. Around your first birthday, you took your first steps and were on your way to faster explorations. You had a few mishaps and wound up on your tush a few times in trying to navigate by yourself, but, eventually, you learned to balance yourself.

The getting from here to there by taking those first baby steps was the first lesson of balance and sequence. Everything else you have done since then has had the very same elements. Today's life is much more than physical movement, however. No matter what goals you choose, you will always have to follow the laws of Balance and Sequence, but the important goals you seek are not of material nature. As we grow and move on to school and other worldly activities, we begin building two artificial systems – belief and value. These are the beasts that will cause us all the pain in our adult lives. We can build a value system in Cogitator, but there is no way a belief can ever get in there. It has to be facts or nothing. Belief implies ignorance. Cogitator uses Boolean algebra and algorithms in its inference engine for its decision-making and maintains only facts, conditions and scenarios on its knowledge base. You can give Cogitator artificial values but false beliefs, no.

There is no organism that does not contain its own Operating System and all operating systems seek only balance. We can call this kind of balance homeostasis, equilibrium, comfort zone or even, Peace of Mind. When the operating system "feels" an out-of-balance condition, it will energize and seek the compensating factor for the condition. Picture a tree on the side of a hill, continually buffeted by the wind. Its operating system has adjusted its growing pattern to compensate for its root position. The beautifully sculpted tree is in balance according to what nature has provided. Why can't people be more like trees? When a person feels an out-of-balance condition, there is no telling what kind of havoc its ego will manifest.

The natural operating system uses Common Sense to make its decisions about its pattern of growth. The ego system uses reasoning to make its decisions. In Cogitator, we separate the elements that cause decisions and assemble the common sense we gave it. Here is part of the description Cogitator: Knowledge can be broken down to its components. They are:

➢ Facts
➢ Activities and processes related to the facts/ restrictions of activities and processes
➢ Context of the facts and processes
➢ Structure supporting the facts

Fact, activity, context, and structure knowledge is collected, stored, and processed according to a learned knowledge collection pattern. Learned data is rationalized, placed into a knowledge-normalized state, and stored in the knowledge base. Knowledge normalization produces a series of facts, related activities, set of contexts, and support structure that describe a common sense scenario.

When we first learn our native language, the above components are the ones we attempt to assign words to in order to "make sense." Facts are akin to nouns we use; activities (or processes) are verbs; context is made of modifiers like adverbs, adjectives, etc. Structure is the environment in which we picture ourselves as inhabiting. We are always within our self-created scenario. As we try and communicate with our environment, we seek balance.

The knowledge base Cogitator builds and uses has no limitations. Another benefit of building knowledge in a machine is that it does not forget. The human ego knowledge base is made up of memories of the body's experiences. Memes make up memories. Most egos have difficulty not only in "re-membering," but also in evaluating those memories. The brain contains these ego memories as traces in its neural networks. Every sensory experience you have necessitates the firing of neurons in your brain that leave trails (much like airliners) and is retained for some period. The larger your knowledge base of experience and the more connections you make, the more ***meaning*** your life has.

The operating system you were born with is the only place you can find truth. There is no external communication that can "teach" you what is true. You may have signposts leading you here and there for achieving mortal goals, but all signposts to the truth point inward.

Communication

Communication: "The sending or receiving of a message that **means the same** to both sender and receiver."

If the above definition is correct, communication in everyday life doesn't happen very often. "Means the same" actually is impossible between people because each individual has his or her own value system for the meaning of any term. This is not the case for a computer, though. Every meaning it handles has to be absolute for every term it handles. If we do not define terms accurately in a computer, it will be the old saw of "Garbage in, Garbage out." We are sentient beings. We have five physical senses that convey our environment to "us" through different rates of vibrations they can sense.

Sense of Touch gives us soft and hard, hot and cold. The molecules of our body pressed against a surface will tell the operating system if we have more or fewer molecules per square inch than the surface (hard or soft) and if its molecules are vibrating slower or faster (cold or hot.)

Sense of Smell differentiates "bad" molecules from "good" molecules in the air. Chemical vibrations that are not conducive to the chemical harmony of our body will repel, while those that are will attract.

Sense of Taste will tell us sweet vibrations from sour vibrations and potentially poisonous substances.

Sense of Hearing receives vibrations from everywhere on a constant basis. When I speak, I am well aware that I am breathing in air, exchanging carbon dioxide with oxygen in my lungs, expelling that air through my vocal cords to create vibrations, modifying those vibrations with my mouth, tongue and teeth to vibrate molecules in the air in such patterns that, when they strike your ear drums and vibrate them in recognizable patterns, they can create the same picture in your mind as is in my mind. We call these kinds of vibrations *language.* Pretty impressive miracle, I think. It is difficult to paint a nice mind picture in someone else's mind with illiteracy.

If you stop and think about what I just said in the above passage, you will immediately know that I didn't SAY anything. The picture of my speaking to you with vibrating air molecules was conveyed to you by the vibrations of the electromagnetic spectrum. They struck the rods and cones of your eyes to create the picture with written words. Is this a wonderful existence, or what?

With the advent of voice recognition software, we can talk to our computers and activate processes with speech. The last time you called a customer service department of a major company, you know you were communicating with a computer for a while. Cogitator resembles the capability of the computer on the Starship Enterprise when Captain Picard says: "Computer..." and the computer responds. This kind of communication exemplifies the capability of Cogitator for the future. Since Cogitator is all about zeroes and ones, there is no language that cannot be replicated in its "mind." Universal translation is around the corner.

Sense of Sight is even more misleading than hearing. Some egos hear what they want to hear; some see what they want to see. The vibrations of the electromagnetic spectrum are many, many times more numerous than those from any other sense - "A picture is worth a thousand words." Just as the listener defines the meaning of the verbal message, the viewer defines the view – "Beauty is in the eye of the beholder." We trust our eyes more than any other sense – "Seeing is believing." The great majority of the human race is blinded, at least in part, by Ignorance.

Sight has been enhanced through the use of telescopes and microscopes. Being able to see things far beyond the capability of human eyes has enabled us to delve deeper and deeper within as well as without. The **Point of View** has access to a much larger view than ever. The wonders of the Universe have never been so exposed in such a glorious manner by today's technology.

Radio and television, as well as cell phones and the Internet have also expanded sight and sound. It is now possible to reach virtually all points of the globe, save for a few wilderness areas, through electronics and radio waves. The Global Positioning System (GPS) can find you anywhere you go when your cell phone has the battery in it and soon, all vehicles will have the same tracking system. Computers have made it happen.

As you read this, you are recognizing the pattern for each letter, each word, and each sentence... and grasp MEANING. (The best you can according to your vocabulary and scope of knowledge.) You compare this Meaning to your own State of Being and decide if it is applicable to you. You seek to harmonize with the message. If the meaning in the message reached your **Common Sense** knowledge and is in harmony with your understanding, you cannot deny it. Truth sticks, but it must first be understood.

These senses gather vibrations from our environment to give their sensory input to our Common Sense, (Soul, Spirit, Mind, etc...) to give us a FEELING of "How am I doing?" **We are walking antennas, both sending and receiving vibratory waves to wend our way through Life.** We are constantly communicating with our **State of Being** by feeling our way. This is Awareness. The response to the vibrations we receive in the echo comes in the form of an "itch to scratch." The Mind sends the instructions in the form of a "desired

State of Being" to the brain for execution of a *routine* (Process of Becoming) to bring back the feeling of "well-being," homeostasis, or Balance. This is where the human ego starts to work.

When ego feels dis-ease, it pays Attention. In this step of thinking, it will take inventory of what it can perceive of the situation, analyze the possible actions to regain homeostasis, prioritize those actions according to its values and beliefs, decide on the best action and either take the action or place it aside for future action. In Cogitator, this is called Finite State Automation. In a human being, it is the *thought cycle*.

Based upon our human knowledge of remedies, neurons in our brain will start firing to make our body change its State of Being (Time, location, circumstances.) We activate the *Process of Becoming*. We regain Balance by visualizing the State of Being we desire. The mind makes it happen by reflecting its State of Being after each thought cycle until the desired balance occurs. We *feel balance* and *think sequence*. Ego sends orders to the brain to activate sequences until the goal is achieved. In Cogitator, this is equivalent to taking pieces of reusable code to build the routine(s) that will service the transaction.

Communicating is all any organism ever does. It is the only thing that makes you *conscious*. Communication is no more than frequencies and amplitudes of vibratory waves of energy in whatever form they take. There are no vibratory waves than cannot be replicated in a computer with sequences of zeros and ones. All human processes and definitions can be stored on knowledge bases and used by Cogitator.

What are we?

"No tragedy can compare with the situation of having our human intelligence – our discerning capacity – channeled, locked away, shut down. This capacity is our greatest treasure, and our one chance for fulfillment."

- From "Time, Space and Knowledge"

Many people will answer quickly when asked **who** they are, but there will be a pause if you ask them **what** they are. Depending upon where you want to stop the description, there are many levels or States of Being we can refer to. For example, you can call yourself a human being, but that does little to tell us what that means. We can call ourselves animals, but that would probably insult most animals. Organism may also fit the bill, but the definition of organism is "living thing." That is no help in defining you.

If we take scientific steps to defining our structure, we can perhaps get a better grip on what we are. (The toe bone is connected to the foot bone, etc.)

We are flesh and blood, bone and marrow and much more than that. We are a combination of the periodic table of elements, from the hydrogen atom with one proton to the explosive and artificial atoms that create bombs to destroy the earth. Each atomic element is in balance in and of itself and can combine with other elements to produce compound molecules. Atoms are comprised of protons, neutrons and electrons. Balance in the atom is provided by a valence electron. This electron is how the atom achieves "equi-valence." All atoms are in a state of equilibrium.

If an atom were the size of an orange, the cloud of electrons that surround it would need space almost as large as a domed football stadium to define their orbits.

If we collapse the electron rings in Mother Earth's matter, she would be about the size of an orange. If we collapse the electron rings in all six billion human beings, they would all fit on the area of a postage stamp. Egos may believe they are substantial, but that certainly is an illusion. That's not all.

Within the atom are other inhabitants. Quarks and quanta, etc. A quantum is a packet of energy. A quark contains either one-third or two-thirds of the electrical energy of the electron. Higher mathematics is the only way to define these tiny beasts. The Grand Unification Theory (GUT) is a quest to try and prove one set of rules for the existence of the universe. This has led to Quantum Mechanics and also spawned the Superstring Theory. Superstrings are thought to be unimaginably small and defined as loops of energy that vibrate and resonate their "being." Their vibrations receive echoes that either attract or repel other Superstrings. There is no such thing as "matter" at this level. Superstrings can pop up anytime. They are the birth of an idea. What we are is an idea. What humans do with this idea is create an ego.

Ah, Dreaded Ego!

Ego looks for humanity
All I seek is Divinity
It's bad enough to work and slave
Ego worries about the grave

It doesn't know Infinity
Has no clue of Eternity
Wants to create Identity
Please go to sleep, nonentity

If Truth were known, we are endless
The past is dead, that's a promise
The future comes as we decide
So come Ego, enjoy the ride

John Stachura – 2004

The ego we create is the only entity that sets value on anything and anyone. What we really are is consciousness looking at itself in a mirror. We live in the equal sign of the existence equation not knowing positive from negative because both sides are equal. That is the real you. The artificial mind that plutocracy indoctrinates into you is the ego most people call Satan.

Zig Ziglar is a "good ol' boy" motivational speaker from Texas who tells stories to illustrate how this ego structure develops.

21

"In the old days, when caravans of circus acts traveled the country, there would be a number of acts in the midway to attract people and separate them from their ready cash. Along the midway would be the Bearded Lady, the Fat Lady, oddities of other sorts and, occasionally, a flea circus."

"When someone wanted to create a flea circus, he would catch a bunch of fleas (there were plenty around in the olden days) and place them in a large jar. The fleas would try to escape by jumping with their extraordinary ability and would hit the sides and top of the jar. The trainer would watch them for a time until the fleas learned exactly where the sides and top were. They would still jump, but stop just short of the surfaces to prevent hurting themselves. Once they were "trained", the trainer could set up a tent and bark at the people walking by to see his "Amazing Trained Flea Circus." He would induce a group to pay their dime and bring them into the tent. There, he would take a cloth off the top of the jar holding the fleas and dump them unto a clean, white tablecloth. They would begin jumping about, but go no further than the limits the jar had set for them. (Oohs and Aahs.)"

Our egos are fleas in jars. Zig asks at the end of this story if listeners would prefer being fleas or flea trainers. My response is to start breaking jars. Egos are trained by experience and the plutocracy to perform within the limits of their own jars. You may have a small jar or a large one, but you will remain a slave to the system for as long as you accept limitations to your real self. If you are willing to have your ego stroked by propaganda and advertising, you are one sorry flea. Inferiority and Superiority complexes indicate Insecurity. There is absolutely no reason for us to make ourselves feel better or worse by comparing our lives to anyone else's.

"The dissenter is every human being at those moments of his life when he resigns momentarily from the herd and thinks for himself."

— Archibald MacLeish

Meditation, imagination and contemplation are the activities that can help us change our minds. There is only one place to go when we want to create a "better" life for ourselves. That is by going within us, not from trying to change our surroundings. We must dissent against propaganda and indoctrination to find our true self because the truth is not what is taught to our children by the existing educational system. We are trained to become fleas that perform the tasks given to us by others. We can still continue to do what we do, but we will never be joyous internally until we understand **why** we do what we do.

Ego is another word for personality. That word comes from the Greek *persona*, which means mask. Mask is an excellent word for ego because all it does is mask the truth we are born with. It gets built from human experience, interaction with others and from the bodily needs that motivate it. It can be described as the knowledge base of experiences the body has weathered. Ego is the only cause of human ills and group egos are the only cause of the world's ills. If we can download this monster into Cogitator and remove the emotion from it, we're on the right path.

Ego Traits

Ego's behavior is dictated by spatial and temporal tendencies. Male egos are territorial because they are more space conscious and female egos are possessive because they are more conscious of time. All egos have all traits, but some traits gain dominance over others because of experience and understanding. Each situation egos face may necessitate a different trait as dominant.

The Myers-Briggs website has many tests to identify personality traits. They basically define the various paths ego may take in processing information. Everyone has all traits in his or her ego. My learning experience with this concept took place when I attended Wilson Learning's "Counselor Selling" class. This is when I was introduced to the Johari Window.

As defined in this class, the Johari window has four quadrants with different personality types in each:

Analytical	Driver
Amiable	Expressive

Top left is the Analytical, top right is the Driver, bottom left is the Amiable and bottom right is the Expressive. Further, in this class, each quadrant is divided again into quadrants of the same names. This creates a sixteen-block grid that mimics the definitions in the Myers-Briggs tests. In the class, these blocks are identified as personality types relating to other personality types. It is a communication window.

I started thinking about this window as how we develop our egos. It made sense that, at the topmost and leftmost point, we begin the age of reason. When we are born, everything we experience relates to us. The word analytical could be shortened to anal, because that is the behavior we first express. Some egos never grow out of this anal stage.

From this block we move our consciousness to the right or downward (into the driver or amiable blocks.) Moving to the right into the driver block is determined by Spatial motivators, also associated with the Type A male dominance behavior. Downward is the Temporal tendency and submissive behavior. I saw the Driver tendency to be right-wing and Amiable as left-wing. Either of these behaviors is out of balance.

The Expressive block piqued my interest. This was the mature ego. One that could maneuver from this block into all other blocks at will. It was the balanced block - the enlightened block. To get into this block, you have to be aware of both spatial and temporal stimuli. You have to be able to turn the coin to ensure there indeed is a head side and a tail side. Another observation that made sense is that this Johari window could have widely different dimensions, based upon knowledge and intelligence. Only the Expressive would have broken his ego jar. The other three blocks are slaves to their skewed thoughts.

Some years later, another thought came to mind. Human egos are indoctrinated into thinking in two-dimensional terms. The Johari window is one of those examples. Spreadsheets are another example. The human existence is three-dimensional and all objectifications are more spherical than linear. If these traits were pictured as being contained in a revolving sphere, (like Momma Earth) reactions to stimuli would be based on ego's attitude at the point of contact. This made much more sense. We all contain the same capability, but the ability to change one's attitude is what truly differentiates levels of understanding.

I contacted Larry Wilson, founder of Wilson Learning, to inform him of this thought. He invited me to be his guest at his Pecos River Learning Center in New Mexico. I was to participate in his "Ropes Course," and experience some of what he was teaching. Near the end of the three days, he asked me to describe what I was talking about. As soon as he understood, his penny dropped and he stopped the goings-on to beckon his entire crew into the room to have me explain this concept to them.

It made sense. All egos contain every trait. Every stimulus is handled according to ego's attitude at the point of communication. Small egos will not adjust their attitude before passing judgment. Mature egos will investigate each stimulus for the best response. The size of your ego jar is defined by your level of understanding.

Ego is motivated by emotion. When you feel something that bothers you, you must activate thoughts to regain the feeling of balance, or homeostasis. Physical balance is one thing you must address with food, water, rest, breathing, etc. However, the emotions that cause the problems in your life are usually those related to intangible sensations - sense of duty, sense of honor, sense of guilt, sense of humor, etc. These types of senses are the ones that throw you out of balance in a way that is difficult to address. The reason is that these particular senses are artificially created by the plutocracy. They are not real, so how can you solve them? The only thing you do when these imaginary values are violated is laugh, cry, or become violent.

"Cogito, ergo sum"
- Rene DesCartes.

This quote is the beginning of DesCartes' effort to prove the existence of God. "I think, therefore, I am" is difficult to grasp, though. There is no questioning the fact that there is something to our existence, simply because it is impossible to ignore our consciousness. If DesCartes had said: "I thinks, therefore, I is," the sentence still makes sense, but assigns consciousness to an "outside" I's existence. If DesCartes had said: "I think, therefore, I am a thinker," it sounds much better to you, right? Said this way, though, it does not establish "being" as the object of the sentence, but "thinker" instead. This sentence also fails in the fact that a thought can be produced by an emotion or imagination. "I think, therefore, I feel" makes much more sense and, even when reversed: "I feel, therefore, I think" works. You think because you feel and you feel because you think. The fact is that, if you are aware, you exist. Because you exist, you will never know what it is to NOT exist. There is no way for you to imagine what nothing (no-thing) is. Nothing is impossible.

Can you imagine for a moment how ridiculous it is to think that you have no life after your body decays? It is just your ego that dies, not the real you. What would be the purpose of gaining consciousness if not to remain conscious? The opposite of life is not death. The opposite of death is birth. Living never stops. Once you can break through your ego jar and see the truth for what it is, you will understand that living for the purpose of dying is not only goofy, but it allows lower mentalities to perform heinous activities.

When I started working for University Computing Company in 1977, this is the first thing I read in "Bits and Pieces."

"It is the end of the sixth day of Creation and God has called his angels together. He addresses the throng:

"Dear angels, we have worked wonders in these last six days." He says. "We have created the Universe with all its galaxies, stars, solar systems and planets and set them all in motion. Here on Earth, we have created a Paradise. We have created mountains and oceans, forests and deserts, plant and animal life and today, my masterpiece, Man, was finished. Tomorrow will be a day of rest, and, from now on, each seventh day will be a day of rest." (Cheers from the multitude.)

He continues. "There is one last thing I must do, however. Man has everything on Earth at his behest and really wants for nothing. I made this masterpiece to appreciate everything we have created for him. In order for him to have the motivation to search this Universe, thereby seeing its wonders, I have decided to hide the Secret of Life from him and I need suggestions for a good hiding place."

A voice from the throng: "Why not place it at the top of the highest mountain on Earth?"

God responds: "Not bad, but man has been made very clever and resourceful. He probably would find it much before he has seen our wonders."

A voice closer in: "Put it at the bottom of the deepest ocean, God."

"That's much better," God replies, "but man will also be developing tools and ways of protecting himself from the elements that may threaten him. Although it would take longer there, he probably still wouldn't be ready for it when he found it."

A tiny cherub at God's knee speaks: "God, why don't you just place it where he would never look?"

"Where would that be, little one?"
"Put it inside him."

Ego is on a constant search for meaning, ignorant of the fact that it is the only entity that creates meaning.

*"Nothing pains some people more
than having to think."*

— Martin Luther King, Jr.

What matters makes sense and what makes sense
matters. Thoughts create what they consider matter and feelings let you know if the matter created by
thought makes sense. The so-called "material" world
you live in is strictly the creation of thoughts. The basic problem with analyzing thought is that there are always two minds trying to do the thinking. We call them
Conscious and Subconscious. You probably will agree
that your waking state is called "conscious" while your
latent one is "subconscious." The conscious is the ego
you use to run your life. Ego, however, is truly subor-
dinate to the subconscious, no matter how ego tries to
glorify itself. What ego does, however, is present goals
to subconscious. Subconscious, being totally apathet-
ic, strives to deliver your conscious desires.

*"Men fear thought as they fear nothing else on
earth – more than ruin – more even than death.
Thought is subversive and revolutionary, destruc-
tive and terrible, thought is merciless to privi-
lege, established institutions, and comfortable
habit. Thought looks into the pit of hell and is
not afraid. Thought is great and swift and free,
the light of the world, and the chief glory of man"*

- Bertrand Russell

In order to understand what a thought is we have to dig deep into ourselves. My thoughts are objectifying themselves on the screen in front of me and they run rampant. Every single keystroke that produced these words was the result of a multitude of thoughts running in a specific sequence. It is a *learned* sequence of thought. Exactly like a computer program. Exactly like the sequence of the DNA double helix. Exactly like what an acorn has "learned" to become an oak tree rather than a Ponderosa pine. Every single thing that exists is a packet of thoughts. There's no such thing as material – just bundles of thoughts. Thoughts that, in effect, become *matter* to us. Sense creates matter and matter makes sense.

When all think alike, then no one is thinking.

— Walter Lippmann

For an in-depth look at your thinking process, try George Boole's (creator of Boolean logic) "The Laws of Thought." If you want further information on one of the founders of modern computerization, use key words "Calculus of Logic" or "George Boole" for the many sites that provide information.

Every thought is *Energy* in motion. Thought creates "E"motion. The Universe is nothing but energy in various manifestations. Einstein certainly showed that everything we call matter could surely return to an energy state. In your bodily state, you are a channel for energy. Your thoughts direct that energy towards the goal(s) you have in mind. If you learn how to control your thoughts, you will achieve anything you place in your mind, given that you commit to it and that it is founded in Truth. It is the thoughts that create the associated effort to reach the goal, not the work itself. You can read as many "How To" books as you wish. The method is not what creates the result. The commitment and focusing on the goal itself is what does it, although the How To may facilitate the journey. Download "As a Man Thinketh" from www.asamanthinketh.net to get another view of this idea.

If you have a well-defined goal in mind, are totally committed to achieving it, and have a clear purpose for the goal, your real mind will take over and bring the necessary elements into your reality to make it happen. You are an energy processor. If you let your ego make the decisions about your material comforts, you are wasting your real power. Picture your mind as a radio. You have different bands of frequencies and amplitudes that bring you the kind of listening you can "tune into." You must stay aware that the one you tune into does not eliminate all other frequencies and amplitudes surrounding your station. So it is with every goal you tune into. The energy flowing through you will make that goal manifest.

A thought is not a thing. It produces a "thing." The thought is a **cycle** that operates in the moment from sense to matter. It then reflects, much like an echo, to see if the matter makes sense. Your life is a reflection of your thoughts. The challenge is finding out how much control you have over your thoughts.

The most important things in life are not things

In trying to visualize a thought, I find the superstring theory to be a good analogy for it. Superstrings are defined as closed loops of energy, provable only through higher mathematics because of their inconceivably tiny size. They vibrate and resonate in various frequencies and amplitudes when they appear. They seek harmony in their echo. That is so poetic. Every thought you have does that and, when you do harmonize with other thoughts, you create a *school of thought* that can be revisited. You place value on this school of thought and file it away in your value system. That is how you collect knowledge.

"Men are not prisoners of Fate, but only prisoners in their own mind."

Franklin D. Roosevelt

A Little History

"There is only one good – knowledge;
and only one evil – ignorance."

Socrates.

Back in the mid-sixties, there was an anecdote being passed around related to computerization. It had to do with scientists creating the then-largest and most powerful computer possible. It was destined to be larger than a city block and taller than the Statue of Liberty. Facts and figures from all sources of knowledge were entered into it for months and months until virtually all the world's libraries had emptied their contents into the behemoth. Organizing and sorting these huge banks of data took additional months but, eventually, the task was done. Now the tests began.

Questions were devised from every discipline known to man and given to the computer for analysis. In every single case, the correct answer was produced. After weeks of this testing, someone had the nerve to formulate a most burning question: "Is there a God?" Gathering themselves before entering the question, scientists eagerly awaited the response. Within a microsecond, the answer came: "There is now!" Twenty years later, the story changed to databases rather than punched cards, but the message was the same. Indeed, if there were an omniscient "god," it wouldn't matter what contained the knowledge.

Trying to understand your intelligence and knowledge and how these elements can be transferred to a machine is what this book is about. The ability to do this exists today, but its usage is subject to interpretation. One way to start examining this process is to go back to the beginning of automation. We must have agreement on the meaning of terms that comprise this concept.

Automation: Making something happen without human intervention; a routine, process, or system that executes to create a predetermined result.

The idea of having machines replicate human functions goes back many years. Blaise Pascal developed a sort of adding machine so that his accountant father could have more time to spend with him. That was in the early 1600's. Probably, George Boole can be credited with kicking the whole thing off in the early to middle 1800's. He established a new branch of mathematics, symbolic logic, in which symbols are used to represent logical operations. In fact, this effort gave birth to Boolean logic. He showed that the symbols of his new mathematics could be made to take on only two values, 0 and 1. This two-valued algebra is what is contained in every single computer operating today. It is the binary numbering system. His ideas of making machines do logic gave birth to the earliest of computers, but it was not Boole who made it happen.

Charles Babbage also had a lot to do with initial computerization. He worked for decades on his Difference Engine that was the precursor for modern computing. Many others in history contributed to the efforts of automating the counting requirements of arithmetic. Ada Lovelace collaborated with Babbage in 1842 by writing an understandable set of instructions that explained how the Analytical Engine he was designing would work. She is thought of by some to be the first computer programmer, although many believe Babbage was the original one.

In 1890, Herman Hollerith developed a system of storing data on cards through the use of punched holes. Each card had 80 columns that could represent numbers from 0 thru 9 and the alphabet. This was the forerunner to unit-record equipment that, for the most part, simply added columns of numbers together and printed their image on paper. In the late fifties and early sixties, things began picking up speed. International Business Machines (IBM) released their first meaningful business computer, the 1400 Series.

The 1401 could read cards, punch cards, print, do arithmetic and compare fields. That was about it. Once a program was assembled, it would be placed in the card reader, preceded by three "bootstrap" cards, and the "Load" button would be pressed for the machine to begin processing. The bootstrap cards contained "hard" instructions that the machine immediately recognized as the beginning of a process. Once these were read into a predetermined area of the CPU, it would activate itself to read the fourth card, fifth card, and so on. If you ever wondered where the term "rebooting" your computer came from, now you know.

Some of the CPU addresses had specific purposes. The card reader would place the contents of a card in addresses 1-80. The cardpunch would punch the contents of addresses 101-180 into output cards and the printer would pick up the contents of addresses 201-332 to print on "green bar" paper. The reason the print line was 132 characters was because this number could be divided into twelve columns of 11 characters each for the accounting people to see a whole year of information on one line. Numbers at that time were not nearly as large as in today's mega-corporations. From this crude beginning, however, the industry rocketed into every aspect of life. It would be impossible to manage any sizable business without automation today.

A major breakthrough in computing power happened in the mid-sixties when IBM announced its System 360. By this time, tape and disk storage had been developed and things were speeding up and growing at a breakneck pace. A new Disk Operating System (DOS) was developed to replace those nasty bootstrap cards and the Autocoder language. This allowed much greater freedom and power to be stored on disk media and be made available to programs as needed. (DOS eventually became MS-DOS when Bill Gates trumped the conservative minds of IBM by acquiring the rights to it and creating Microsoft.) New programming languages were created to make better use of the new technologies and systems. The new frontier let go of "data processing" and went into "Information Systems."

The really significant change in this move was the usage of the binary system instead of the Hollerith code. IBM now used hexadecimal (base-16) numbering in its CPUs. Each byte exploded in potential. At the bottom of base-16, base-32 or base-64, etc. is the binary system of 0 and 1. Automation took off.

Standardization was becoming an issue. Many large companies had hundreds of programmers who were still pretty independent and innovative. Some companies made commitments to specific programming languages and corralled the talent pool for the language chosen. Sears, for example, had over four hundred PL/1 programmers in the late sixties and early seventies. That was one reason they were inflexible and slow to change. Almost all large companies were migrating to Common Business-Oriented Language (COBOL) by this time and stodgy Sears never recovered from its close-minded way of doing business. In those days, Sears would force their vendors to do things the way they wanted, which was usually dictated by the shortcomings of Sears' computer systems.

The conservative mind of American Business was evident across the country. Decisions to stay put with existing systems became corporate suicide. This is quite evident today as corporations gobble up competition that is unable to change fast enough. If the executives at Sears had any imagination, there would be no Wal-Mart today. In the seventies, there was little or no competition and sales for Sears were greater than today. Meanwhile, Wal-Mart became six or seven times bigger in sales numbers.

System/360 also introduced databases. IBM's Information Management System (IMS) was touted as the new way to store and access data. This was a hierarchical database, meaning that all data had levels of importance in the entire structure. This was very similar to a Bill of Material for a company's information system. A Bill of material in manufacturing is like a component list of a do-it-yourself kit. It identifies all the parts required to put a product together and how they are connected. A Data Dictionary was developed to try and track all pieces of information for the users to be able to find what was needed to process information. Specialists had to be used due to the complexity of this approach. Very few companies ever developed this product to its full potential. By the time people started to understand how to use this database, relational databases were surfacing.

Whereas IMS had a rigid structure, relational databases gave great freedom for users to link data together. They eventually led to Knowledge Bases, which then began to feed Intelligent Systems. Today, huge systems are common and the personal computer has empowered individuals to perform tasks that were not imagined in the sixties. The Internet has linked millions of users together with unlimited knowledge available at the click of a mouse. The reason relational databases exploded is because they mirror the workings of the human brain. Data can be linked to many other pieces of data to create information. When you put pieces of data together in the proper sequence, you wind up with data "*in formation.*"

The quest for Artificial Intelligence began in the thirties. Many attempts have been made to bring this concept to computerization. Alan Turing, developer of the Turing Test, probably evidences the best effort. One of the problems in trying to create this kind of environment is that Intelligence cannot be artificial. Artificial means man-made and real intelligence cannot be man-made. The definition is misleading. It is possible to make Artificial Knowledge, but intelligence is constant. Everything contains the intelligence to be what it is. We should be on a quest for Wisdom. Wisdom can be measured by how well your intelligence uses the knowledge you have acquired. Cognitor calls this Common Sense.

Experience from applying the Cogitator engine and from further product designs has indicated the direction of the ontology for common sense reasoning. Learning and the content of learning create a knowledge-normalized knowledge base that includes the following common sense factors:

- ➢ Facts
- ➢ Activities and processes related to the facts / restrictions of activities and processes
- ➢ Context of the facts and processes
- ➢ Technical structure supporting the facts

Fact, activity, context, and structure knowledge is collected, stored, and processed according to a learned knowledge collection pattern. Learned data is rationalized, placed into a knowledge-normalized state, and stored in the knowledge base. Knowledge normalization produces a series of facts, related activities, set of contexts, and support structure that describe a common sense scenario. Ultimately the use of the knowledge needs to be timely. Speed of use is accomplished from normalizing the data and creating reusable, quantified knowledge.

The engine uses algorithms to capture knowledge and to make recommendations from the knowledge. The algorithmic use of reusable knowledge, and scenarios make it possible to accomplish identified goals including:

- ✓ Problem resolutions
- ✓ Recommended activities and settings
- ✓ Recommended studies to resolve unknown settings
- ✓ List required actions in criticality order

Recommended activities or restrictions on activities are a learned process. They are an extension to the problem and resolution environment. Given a common set of data and a state requiring a decision, the set of facts is interpreted (including application of laws of physics or software applications) and a process selects the specific action recommendation.

The above passages come from a description of Cogitator and the inference engine. If you can understand it, you are among the chosen few. The first understanding we must come to is that all programs and systems work the same way. One of the easiest ways to relate to any system is to compare it to making a meal. All recipes have ingredients required for the final product, preparation of the individual components that go into the meal, and cooking the mixture into what is to become a savory delight. Systems have inputs and processes that act upon those inputs to create the eventual output. Just like our morning routine is a recipe for preparing our bodies for public display. All have a specific goal to be reached by the actions performed on the ingredients required. There is no other way of describing any system. The difference in the output is based on executing the instructions in the right sequence and the skill and knowledge applied during the process. The same recipe can yield vastly different results depending on who is doing the cooking.

Cogitator knows this. It doesn't care what the names of the ingredients are. It only knows they are ingredients for a particular recipe. It cares about the goal to be reached, **when** it needs to be reached, **what** ingredients are used in the process and the knowledge pieces it needs to perform the task(s). It puts them all together in the proper sequence to achieve the goal. This is called a **scenario**. If used in a business, for example, it needs to be taught what financial goals it has to work on and how to prioritize those goals. The ingredients and knowledge already exist in the organization. Cognitor, Inc. can start transforming the lines of code into a knowledge base one piece at a time until the whole organization has everything connected and aimed at the same goal. As the company evolves and wants to make changes, only the knowledge and goals need to be changed to change the Corporate "Mind." This would remove the need for code maintenance and reduce IT budgets tremendously.

There are many similarities in any software system and our own human makeup. What programs do is achieve an end result. All programs work the same way, whether in a machine or a human being. Any operating system in a computer works the same way as the operating system we were born with. All learning begins with communication. Communication is "the sending or receiving of a message that **means the same** to both sender and receiver." The message contains knowledge. If that knowledge **makes sense**, it becomes learned. We all contain the knowledge of what it is to be a human being and that knowledge can be encapsulated in the zeroes and ones of a knowledge base in a computer. There are no limits to knowledge. In a machine, it is "normalized" onto a knowledge base, just as our own learned knowledge is stored in our DNA and modified by our experiences. The same elements exist in both.

Definitions in Cogitator are divided into facts, activities, context and structure. This is equivalent to a manufacturing Bill of Material for a product. A Bill of Material is similar to a component and instruction kit for putting something together. Model airplane kits do this and Heathkit of the past used to have kits for virtually any whim. The instruction manual for these kits is just like a Bill of Material. This allows the software to recognize, analyze, categorize, harmonize, and energize to create the result required. Just like a human being does it. Beauty is in the "ize" of Cogitator. Its Bill of Material is made up of thoughts converted to zeros and ones.

In a computer, all that is known is represented by sequences of zeros and ones. In a human being, these sequences are vibrations of varying frequencies and amplitudes. There is nothing ego "knows" that Cogitator cannot also know.

Use of knowledge is based upon a Value System. Computers will prioritize their actions and execute instructions based upon what human beings define to it. Human beings prioritize their actions based upon what they think they know and understand. Unfortunately, human beings also carry a Belief System within their ego and this is the faulty element that causes all human ills. In business, all functions being executed in the daily work are well defined and "known" to someone. Again, though, showing the same report to more than one person will normally cause that report to be interpreted differently because people have different Points of View in evaluating any stimulus.

To get knowledge into a knowledge base should be the objective of any "intelligent" system. Getting a grasp on what all this means necessitates a much deeper understanding of what we are. If we are to mirror human functions in a machine, we have to know how ego functions.

Ego Mind

"Those who would give up essential liberty to purchase a little temporary safety deserve neither liberty nor safety."

Benjamin Franklin

There are many different States of Mind. Every Being is a State of Mind. Since Mind is spiritual energy, all beings are spiritual energy in the process of reconstitution. There is nothing more certain than the fact that energy is always in motion and in a state of evolution. The most harmful mind existing is the Mind Set that egos cling to. Once the mind sets (like concrete) it becomes an obstacle to the natural development of mind. Spiritual energy is in constant motion, so when it encounters a mindset, something has to give. Mindsets are ego jars and are the only cause of pain, violence and man's inhumanity to man.

The Open Mind is the savior. This is the Liberal Mind, whereas the Mind Set is the conservative. Liberal means tolerant, generous and normally, kind. Conservative means "I want to keep all I have and not share it with anyone." Conservatives prefer censors and political "correctness" (which is simply artful lying,) and will resist change until death. They seek to impose their way of living onto others, but only if they can control the money, as well. Conservative egos can be considered the best example of the neighborhood bully. They rule the media with right-wing fanatics like Rush Limbaugh and Paul Harvey and laugh on their hypocritical way to the bank. They spout morality and send soldiers to kill or be killed.

All conservatives are fleas in jars. They have stopped seeking knowledge and meaning in their lives. They are already dead and just waiting for someone to let them know so they can step into the grave. They are control freaks that know how to jerk the reins, but have no idea where to go. The basic difference between a liberal mind and a conservative mind is that conservatives focus on methods and liberals focus on goals. All methods are faulty to some degree.

"While the State exists, there can be no freedom. When there is freedom, there will be no State"

Lenin

"State" comes from the word **stasis**, which is defined as motionless or inert. The word is constantly used to describe solidified thoughts in all aspects of human situations. The United *States*, for example, imply that different geographic areas have different laws. The State of the Union address supposedly is telling us what shape the country is in. State can also be a state of homeostasis or equilibrium, in which two opposing sides create a balance point for each other. The balance point is the equivalent of the equal sign in an equation. This is evidenced in business as Assets and Liabilities, in politics as Liberal and Conservative, in humans as Male and Female, Yin and Yang, etc. Since there is no such thing as **motionless**, all states of being are examples of two complementary sides seeking balance with each other.

Ego trying to understand life is like a blood corpuscle wondering where the circulatory system begins and ends as it travels through the veins and arteries. We are always in a *state of becoming*, not in a *state of being*. Ego wants to create beginnings and ends, but these do not exist in reality. *Living* is a verb and ego wants to make *life* a noun. Another absolute law to add to balance and sequence is that we are in a constant state of *evolution*. Ego stops time to check its feelings every once in a while and imagines beginnings and ends, but there are none except in the artificial world ego creates.

How does ego check its feelings? The human body has five physical senses to compare itself against the environment. Non-physical senses like sense of balance, sense of sequence, sense of humor, sense of honor, etc. also affect decisions made by ego. All senses transfer their information to the mind by *communicating* a value of what they sense. This is the only way a decision can be made. Depending on an individual ego's value system, the same communication may create a different decision in another ego. Your natural mind will attempt to deliver on whatever decision your ego makes.

All senses seek balance, homeostasis, or equilibrium. These words have the same meaning. They create ego's "*comfort zone.*" In Cogitator, definitions are absolute, but using probability theory can artificially create feelings. This is similar to entering a search argument in any Internet search engine. Those sites with the highest percentage of similarities will be listed for you. (Probable results.) If the computer's knowledge base cannot quite recognize some sense (transaction,) it can ask a user for help in identifying it. This is similar to learning how to wash your hands when you were small. If after you learned how to wash your hands, your mom told you to wash your face, you may have asked if it was similar to washing your hands. If she said yes, you went ahead and *learned* how to wash your face. Each learning experience adds a brick to your knowledge base. Likewise, if you interact with Cogitator, it will learn from you.

The human body has needs to maintain its current existence. Among these are food, water, etc. These primary movers are what ego has to make decisions about every single day. In short, you prioritize your actions in your life according to what you consider **most important at this time, in this place, under these circumstances.** In Cogitator, these conditions are called *scenarios.* Every human ego deals with scenarios at every waking moment and each scenario is the most important in that ego's life. You are always seeing life working on its number one priority – **always.**

Value systems are processed by ego pretty much as Abraham Maslow depicted in his Hierarchy of Needs in 1949. Ego prioritizes the actions in your life according to importance assigned by your value system.

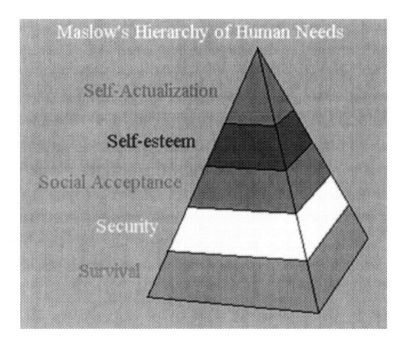

These five "S" needs create the priority sequence of your actions, according to Maslow. You cannot proceed to the top without having met the lower level needs. For example: if you feel you do not have social acceptance, you will not gain self-esteem. If there ever was a picture of how ego tries to create a reality for itself, this is as close an approximation as you can find. As with most depictions, however, it offers a skewed view of actuality.

First, there are no straight lines in the universe. Pyramids suggest climbing and struggle. The ego persona is more like a sphere, or a superstring. If you can imagine Maslow's pyramid to be spherical and look at the levels of attainment as layers of protection, (similar to an onion) and the tip of the pyramid as the core of your consciousness, you will have a better idea of what you need to do to reach your true self. This pyramid of needs is fine and dandy for interaction in the material world, but there seems to be a lack of further definition beyond that world. It appears to be what ego needs, rather than what the real person within needs. If you were truly enlightened, you would know that life is eternal and survival would not even be a concern. On that conjecture, the entire pyramid crashes into meaninglessness. However, from a day-to-day standpoint, it is close to reflecting how most people would prioritize their To Do List.

The problem with this pyramid hierarchy though, is that it is based on the selfish motives of ego. It is probably accurate as you try to develop an identity, but it certainly ignores the deeper, actual being. For now, though, Maslow's pyramid is a good point to start examining your ego. The third level (social acceptance) is the one the plutocracy controls with its laws and policies. It is supposed to be civilization, but it is primarily used to enforce rules based upon the plutocrats' wishes. Because the herd instinct is very strong in humans, it works pretty well.

There is another way of looking at your mind's universe. It can be likened to fractals. Benoit Mandelbrot created the first fractal while he was working for IBM.

Mandelbrot Set
Polish-born French mathematician Benoit Mandelbrot coined the term "fractal" to describe complex geometric shapes that, when magnified, continue to resemble the shape's larger structure. This property, in which the pattern of the whole repeats itself on smaller and smaller scales, is called self-similarity. The fractal shown here, called the Mandelbrot set, is the graphical representation of a mathematical function.

Tony Stone Images/Stephen Johnson

Microsoft ® Encarta ® 2006. © 1993-2005 Microsoft Corporation. All rights reserved.

At the center of the image above is a three-dimensional geometric fractal. When this fractal was first released, you could get a thirty-minute video that showed the internal structure. There are an infinite variety of fractals visible on the web. They all resemble the echo of self-similarity as though the formulas were Superstrings resonating to themselves. Consciousness can create any such universe.

If you want to explore how you think, there are tests you can give yourself. There are a number of them at www.similarminds.com that can give you insight as to how your mind compares to others. Another worthwhile test site is www.humanmetrics.com. These can only give you some idea of where you are in comparison with your neighbors. It is up to you to take charge of your thoughts and begin transforming your ego. Once you begin your quest, I guarantee you will become a different person. Take yourself seriously and be totally honest with your thoughts, feelings and actions and "Mastery of Life" will be yours.

Decisions,
Decisions, Decisions

"Knowing others is wisdom. Know-
ing the self is enlightenment. "

— Lao-tzu

When I first started programming the IBM 1400 series, the language I used was Autocoder. The most powerful instruction in that language was the Compare instruction. When the program compared two fields, there were three possibilities for where it would go to (branch) next. These possibilities were routines to continue processing based upon the two fields being compared as equal or one was higher than the other in value. When programs and systems were designed these "decisions blocks" would be drawn in a Flow Chart to define visually what the program would do internally. That is still how programs work today, even though the language may differ.

In COBOL, (COmmon Business Oriented Language) the IF command replaced the Compare of Autocoder. Many programmers, including myself, would use "nested IFs" to create more complex decisions in the same routine. These methods are the exact same way the ego makes decisions. Whatever you will do in the next moment is created by this constant comparison within your value system.

Value systems exist only in ego, but there are many varieties of ego. Individual egos can get themselves in balance if they try, but there are also collective egos to deal with in society. Many decisions made by individuals are based upon the values that society has given them. The prevalent value society gives you to use is the dollar. Making people want money is how society controls most of the population. It appears that many people equate success with money. Of course, that is not how you will find joy, but ego gets a kick from having lots of money.

The decision is the lowest common denominator of human action. It is said that humans have will power, but this is untrue. The only thing that the human ego can actually decide is to NOT do what should be done under the circumstances. Ego has "won't" power. The natural operating system always wants balance. Ego is the only element that creates out-of-balance conditions. Those out-of-balance conditions are what the plutocracy uses to manage the herds. This is done by assigning values to elements that really have no value in truth - like money.

A decision is made when ego's homeostasis is threatened. The goal of the decision is to regain it. If you get up in the morning and create a To Do List, those items on it are for you to maintain equilibrium for the day. Each item is a goal. For you to regain control over your life, you must become aware of the decisions you are making and WHY you are making them. You must be able to differentiate whether a decision is made to advance your understanding of life or to simply be a cog in the wheel of "The System." If you stay in your ego jar, you are a slave to the system.

I was introduced to the Rosicrucians by an ad in the now-defunct Omni magazine. They advertised a course called "Mastery of Life" and gave contact information. With a course title like that, I couldn't see how anyone could resist. For three years, I received monographs in the mail explaining how consciousness happens. If you want to break your ego jar, look into this.

In 1989, I read "Time, Space and Knowledge" by Tartang Tulku of Dharma Publishing. According to this book, there are two levels of these three elements of consciousness. They are separated into Great Time, Great Space and Great Knowledge as opposed to Ordinary Time, Ordinary Space and Ordinary Knowledge. To me, this indicated the Great as the natural Operating System and the Ordinary as ego Operating System. There are over thirty exercises in this book for you to delve deep into your consciousness. The web site is probably the best place to go. If you can understand even half of what is taught there, your ego jar has no chance of survival.

"Since everything is but an apparition perfect in being what it is, having nothing to do with good or bad, acceptance or rejection, one may as well burst out in laughter."

- Longchenpa

The plutocracy wants you to make decisions. It will also give you the belief and value systems with which to make those decisions. It will take polls and surveys to ensure there are enough of you agreeing on their way of thinking. If the polls indicate dissent, the message will change, but the method of control will not. This is all done with indoctrination, propaganda, misinformation, disinformation and downright lies.

The best tool the plutocracy has today to maintain control over ego minds is the television. Have you noticed the viewing audience voting in the current "reality" shows like American Idol, Dancing With the Stars, and the like? These shows tell the plutocracy how many asses and dolts they can easily manipulate.

Your decision is the ONLY point of control you have. No one can make a decision for you unless you give up your "capacity to discern." If you mindlessly turn on the television each morning, you are a mind slave to the system. If all you do is work to create money and take no time to understand the value of YOU, you are a slave to the system. If you believe that our leaders are here to take care of you, ditto. Wake up!

> ***"We should stop kidding ourselves. We
> should let go of things that aren't true.
> It's always better with the truth."***
>
> ***R. Buckminster Fuller***

"Bucky" Fuller's embraced the Gaea Theory that the Earth is an organism and we are simply a microcosm of that organism in human form. Also, anything that is contained within us is a microcosm of ourselves. Without doubt, Buckminster Fuller was a visionary and creative genius. Much more information about his works is at www.bfi.org.

Imagination

"Within you right now is the power to do things you never dreamed possible. This power becomes available to you just as soon as you change your beliefs."

Dr. Maxwell Maltz

When you imagine something within yourself, it must be possible. If you attempt to use language and ego terms to describe some image, it will be difficult. There is no way for the power that drives you to create something not possible in your mind. Only ego can lie. If you can think it, you can do it. Imagination, however, can only be the motivator for your actions. It cannot make you *do*. It is up to you to surround yourself with the circumstances that will define who you want to be. The only way to achieve any imagined goal is to make the **decision** to do it. Making a decision is the lowest common denominator of achievement. Do you REALLY want what you imagine? If so, then make the decision to commit your efforts to achieving it.

"Imagination continually frustrates
tradition; that is its function."

— John Pfeiffer

If you want to imagine yourself healthy, will you make the decision to avoid what gives you dis-ease? The only way you feel dis-ease is because you imagine dis-ease. Think healthy and let your decisions focus on that goal. If you want to imagine wealthy, forget about money and focus on helping others to be wealthy. They will provide you with anything you need and perhaps more. Don't be greedy. If you want to imagine yourself wise, focus on removing the lies and beliefs that have caused you pain. You were born perfect with all the knowledge you need encoded in your DNA. Look inside for the truth. It is the only place you will ever find it. The difference between training and education is simple. Training is indoctrination of a method to achieve a goal. Education is to bring the best method from within. Trust yourself. However, in order to trust yourself, you must know yourself.

"When I examine myself and my methods of thought, I come close to the conclusion that the gift of fantasy has meant more to me than my talent for absorbing positive knowledge."

— Albert Einstein

One reason for so many people joining the herd, rather than controlling their own life, is the desire to belong. If you can recall Maslow's pyramid, you will see that social acceptance is normally the next thing ego seeks after Survival and Security. You can equate this level with the sex drive and the desire to create "families." Very few people will ever rise above this level. The fact is that, if you have food, water, shelter and sex, what motivation is given you to seek the source of your existence? Most people are lost in the forest and do not know which direction leads out.

Imagine yourself being more than a body. Imagine being a self-sustainable universe unto yourself. What would you do with the power of creating your own universe? Screw being king of the world. Be the lord of the universe. Why don't you break your jar and do it?

"The problems of the world cannot possibly be solved by skeptics or cynics whose horizons are limited by obvious realities. We need men and women who can dream of things that never were."

- John F. Kennedy

Motivation is the cause for making your decisions. When you were a child and you did something that your parents did not like, they may have asked you why you did it. Do you remember saying: "be-cause?" There is a cause for each and every one of your actions. You do things because you are motivated. The reason you are motivated is because you are stimulated to do so.

Before you ever drove a car, you saw others driving a car. You imagined the day when you would be old enough to drive your own car. Do you drive now? Before you ever owned a house, you saw others living in homes and imagined owning your own home. Do you live in your own home now? When you imagine yourself being healthy, wealthy and wise, do you think anything can stop you from achieving that? Only you can stop you.

It is not what you own that defines who you are. It is what you are that defines what you own. The truth of the matter is that you will never own anything. The plutocracy may give you license to say you "own" something, but that license can be removed at any time and, certainly, when you realize that you take nothing with you when you depart the physical world, this truth is evident. The number of people who are willing to empower you best measures success and wealth. When you imagine yourself to be the person you were born to be, all elements that allow that to happen will come together for you. Who is that person? What would that person do? The only way to really find out is to "leggo your ego." You must delve into yourself for the answers without accepting what you consider your "external" observations.

There is more purpose in living on earth than to pass time until you depart. If you believe that your time on earth is meant to be nothing more than preparing for your death, you are already dead. The evolution of our species is transcending the material concept of our human senses and taking us into the creative world of metaphysics. Every imagined result will occur if you release the erroneous beliefs you have been taught. Every belief is at least partially false. Imagine knowing the truth.

"Imagination is more important than knowledge."

— Albert Einstein

Imagination is the only source of creativity. It is the only way to find ways of cleaning up our planet, ending all violence and strife, and making Mother Earth the Garden of Eden once again.

John Lennon had it in a nutshell:

Imagine there's no heaven
It's easy if you try
No hell below us
Above us only sky
Imagine all the people
Living for today...

Imagine there's no countries
It isn't hard to do
Nothing to kill or die for
And no religion too
Imagine all the people living life in peace...

You may say I'm a dreamer
But I'm not the only one
I hope someday you'll join us
And the world will be as one

Imagine no possessions
I wonder if you can
No need for greed or hunger
A brotherhood of man
Imagine all the people

Sharing all the world...

You may say I'm a dreamer
But I'm not the only one
I hope someday you'll join us
And the world will live as one

Imagine the nightly news stating that all people are actually good. Imagine not being bombarded by advertising to buy items of no value. Imagine honesty contests, instead of American Idol. Imagine no borders on the face of the planet. How could we go to war if there were no borders? The Beatles' John Lennon knew these things. Imagine not giving power to those who use it for their own benefit. Imagine loving your neighbor as yourself. Imagine living the Golden Rule. Imagine creating your future because you can.

"Imagination is the beginning of creation. You imagine what you desire, you will what you imagine and at last you create what you will"

George Bernard Shaw

Imagine Peace. True peace, not some temporary truce. If, as you read these words, you can actually commit to making a change from what you currently are, you have taken the first step. It is not you who will change from what you truly are. It is the circumstances around you that will change for what you want them to be. Just be yourself and express your new image to those around you. All the detractors will move away from you and your conviction and only the supporters of your new self will remain. You have arrived already if you plant this in your mind and focus all your energy on the image of your dreams. Only your false beliefs will slow you down.

Imagine heaven. Imagine being in heaven. Are you not already there? You may point towards the sky to imagine heaven, but Australians are pointing in the opposite direction. There very probably is another life form in the universe pointing towards you and calling this place you occupy "heaven." You have to let go of fantasy if you want to control your life. The truth is simple: you create your own heaven or hell.

Ignorance and Apathy

*"I have never let my schooling
interfere with my education"*

Mark Twain

The only reason you do not have everything you dream of is because of Ignorance and/or Apathy. Stop. Think. What is the difference between Ignorance and Apathy? "I don't know and I don't care!" All of us know some things and care somewhat, but the level of each differs from person to person. The only thing that causes fear is ignorance and knowledge is the only way to remove it. Apathy is caused by lack of caring, or loving. Love transcends all Being and is absolutely necessary for enlightenment to occur. This love is the kind of love that Buddha demonstrated and Jesus taught as *agape*, selfless and spiritual love.

> ## *"Education is a progressive discovery of our own ignorance"*
>
> ### *Will Durant*

Ignorance causes fear. It is the only thing that causes fear. Almost all human activity on this planet is caused by fear. The biggest fear is Fear of Death and all other fears are based on this. If we do not fear death, we cannot have other fears. What does not kill us will strengthen us. We can indoctrinate people to remove the Fear of Death by having them believe that Paradise is attainable through sacrifice, but that is only brainwashing. If the ruling class really believed we could reach some other form of life that would reward us for sacrificing our own, they would be the first in line. They use Ignorance to sacrifice others.

The second greatest fear is Fear of Pain. Most people have low pain thresholds and try to avoid the experience, but we can either bear the pain or our mind will put our body to sleep. The third greatest fear is Fear of Punishment. Those in power manipulate the ignorant through the use of these fears. All these fears are created by ego in its attempts to establish itself as "real." If we know the truth about what causes these fears, they will go away. We cannot fear what we understand.

Ignorance is the strongest motivator used by the plutocracy to maintain control. If Ignorance is the only thing that causes Fear, then Knowledge is the only thing that can eliminate it. If we do not seek knowledge, we can never activate ourselves for our own benefit. The plutocracy that creates the "fear factors" will control our thoughts and emotions for as long as we hang on to the thought that "someone else" is better than we are or knows more than we do.

Newspapers, magazines, movies, television and governments all press the security issue to make us fear even going to the grocery store. Tabloids try to sell the idea that our "idols" are better off than we are and tout them to be above the herd. They are actually picked by the herders to make us feel as though they would do this for anyone in the herd. They drive us as a herd to wherever they want us to be. So much of what the plutocrats do is stamped "Top Secret" that you know they are plotting something for their own benefit.

"To fear is to fear life, and those who fear life are already three parts dead."

— Bertrand Russell

You can only be manipulated by your Ignorance. If you are willing to accept what others tell you as truth, then you have not yet looked in the right place. It is "knowingness" that will allow you to understand what "godness" is. The State of Being that is Knowingness is the divine knowledge of Jesus and Buddha. Knowingness will transcend the human ego and unify it with the real Self and with the Eternity of Time and the Infinity of Space. Your ego can be "in tune" with these thoughts, if it is willing to let go of the lies that created it.

"To be conscious that you are ignorant is a great step to knowledge."

Benjamin Disraeli

Ego is quite a stubborn entity. It is an artificial mind that is constructed by human experience and indoctrination. It begins to rear its ugly head at an early age, especially in the Western World, when you are taught that you are "different" or "unique." Only ego seeks to differentiate itself from the real existence of divine Being. It is the only element that causes the world's problems. It is your own personal Satan. To rid yourself of this stigma, you must learn what lies it tells you and start replacing them with truth. You must peel your onion. Once the layers of ego are removed, your real Self will be free to emerge.

"The realization of ignorance is the first act of knowing."

— Jean Toomer

Many people confuse Knowledge with Intelligence. Knowledge contains the puzzle pieces that Intelligence puts together to create a wise decision. In "The Archaeology of Knowledge," Michel Foucault suggests that the knowledge of the universe is encoded in us at birth. All we need do is look inside ourselves for the answers we seek. It truly is contained in the double helix of our DNA. We are, in fact, an embodiment of knowledge necessary to be a human being.

The Greek word Cognos means knowledge. When we "cognize" something, we know it. When we re-cognize something, we find what was always there within us. We make *dis*-coveries. We remove the falsehoods to see the truth that had been covered. That's what happened to me on that February 8 in 1982.

Intelligence Quotient is not a measure of ability. It is a measure of time. The puzzle is put together *__faster__* with higher IQ, but everyone can put the puzzle together. When higher intelligence is given tougher puzzles, it doesn't give up. It simply looks deeper into the innate, encoded knowledge until the answer appears. Weaker minds will be distracted by the next stimulus before the solution arrives. The best measure of intelligence is the ability to *focus attention* and hold a thought until complete.

> **"It's not that I'm so smart, it's just that I stay with problems longer."**
>
> **- Albert Einstein**

In order to navigate your way through this world, you must have human experience to make decisions and partake of what this life has to offer. However, it is not the material world that will give you Peace of Mind. You can look at "successful" people by what their material possessions are, but this is a shallow success.

> **"The human thought must free itself from self-imposed materiality and bondage."**
>
> **-From "Science and Health" by Mary Baker Eddy.**

Ego seeks to align itself with other egos in order to justify its existence. Two or more egos that agree with their individual beliefs will create a group ego or culture. These can be found in clubs, corporations, governments, and the like. These group egos are far more powerful than individual egos because they tend not to listen to another point of view when confronted about their beliefs. The fact that it is discouraged to discuss religion and politics in many countries is because it would make people think about what they believe. The plutocracy doesn't like an educated herd. There's too much chance for revolution if people wise up to the truth. The plutocrats would still have you believe the earth is flat.

"Ignorance is not bliss—it is oblivion."

- Philip Wylie

The educational systems of the West do not educate. Education comes from the word "educe." To educe means, "to draw out," and this is not what is being done in our schools today. Training is the injection of a program, or routine, into ego mind to be performed as needed. This is indoctrination. Indoctrination is what is being done in our schools. The same applies to the churches, synagogues, mosques and temples and the rot they train into you. These institutions and the governments they spawn are the cause of the pain the world feels today.

"It is only to the individual that a soul is given."

Albert Einstein

Mind control, (or Ego control) has become relatively simple with today's communication systems and endless electronic toys. Keep the herd busy with nonsensical activity and make sure it is well fed, so that it cannot know when it will be sent to slaughter. Keep producing shows and movies that strengthen sex and violence in society, display sports that serve up gratuitous violence in large portions, etc. Divide and conquer by using the herd's ignorance against itself. Terms like "National Security" really mean security for the plutocracy, not the herd. Having secrets and the power to withhold information from the herd certainly indicates shady dealings. There are no secrets that indicate something good is being hidden. Just the opposite.

"No darkness like ignorance."

North African saying

People want to believe their group is right so that they can justify their ego's actions. Unfortunately, no group ego can ever be better than an individual Self. The purpose for injecting false beliefs into individuals is to control them and prevent them from thinking "outside the box." Fear is the normal method for the plutocracy to make the herd move in the direction it wants it to go. If you take a close look at the politics of the day, you will find that most people are concerned with what the government is telling them. They have no concept whatsoever that they created the government that creates their problems. There is no finger pointing that ever solved anything. We are all responsible.

"The ideals which have always shone before me and filled me with the joy of living are goodness, beauty and truth. To make a goal of comfort or happiness has never appealed to me; a system of ethics built on this basis would be sufficient only for a herd of cattle."

Albert Einstein

"Stupid is forever, Ignorance can be fixed."

Don Wood

Forget what is happening around the world and start working on what is happening inside you. That's where everything begins and ends. Stop pointing fingers away from yourself and start digging deep into the mind you were born with. You CAN make a difference! The reason for your apathy is because you feel helpless. Start being helpful. Is it that important to swill beer and munch on potato chips while watching some spectacle of violence like the Super Bowl? Can you no longer get a thrill from learning something that can improve your life? Are you going to stay hypnotized by the advertisers who want you to move money? Don't even try to convince anyone that you are happy doing that. You are a zombie, if you do.

"Violence is the last refuge of the incompetent"

Isaac Asimov

Have you ever considered why you are prejudiced? Is it because of your personal experience or is it because you were indoctrinated that way? If there should be prejudice, it possibly could be based on blood type. If you need a blood transfusion to stay alive, would it really matter who donated the pint that saved your life? Think about it. Do you honestly believe that you are better than any other life that has been given to any other being? Stop and think. All the plutocracy wants to do is to make you believe that they know what is best for you. Isn't that a total farce? Stop and think. If you insist on being a follower, at least follow the leaders that can improve the situation.

Many people hand over their lives to the plutocrats without knowing what they can do for themselves and by themselves. It basically gives the "leaders" license to take advantage of ignorance. Why you would want to have someone else do your thinking for you is a mystery. The reason why you hand your life to someone else is because you do not have any idea how to manage it yourself. You have become dependent upon what the plutocracy provides and have little or no idea how to live without the comforts you have available. There is no reason to give your power to someone else unless you are totally clueless about life. It is time to wake up.

"There is only one good – knowledge;
and only one evil – ignorance."

Socrates.

There is a huge gap of knowledge between the average person and the providers of information. Extremely sophisticated advances in virtually all fields of endeavor have been made possible by the computer, but most people have little or no idea how things are done or produced in the modern age. It is not easy for most people to contemplate the "Big Picture." The most disturbing aspect of this powerful technology is not that it can harm people, but that people can use it to harm others. Just like the atomic bomb, actually.

Where is this technology leading us? In the computer age, more advances in knowledge have been made than all of previous history. This has been caused by the continual improvement of computerization. From a CPU of 8K capacity in 1963, I am now typing on a personal computer that is less than one percent the size of that 1401 and contains 128 MEGABYTES capacity! That is sixteen thousand times the computing power contained in about one percent of the space. What will the next forty years bring if this exponential evolution revolution continues? The physical world is no longer the limit of knowledge. We are now exploring the inner self and considering spiritual growth as the only way to develop further.

"Fear always springs from ignorance."
— Ralph Waldo Emerson

In "Time, Space and Knowledge," Tarthang Tulku suggests that these three elements define our consciousness and universe. Tulku, a Buddhist lama, founded Dharma Publishing in California after spending five years in India. He had escaped Tibet when the Chinese were seeking to purge the Buddhist hierarchy there. His first effort was to compile the 108 books comprising Buddhist texts. In this book (TSK, for short,) he provides 35 meditation exercises to delve deep into the mind. He differentiates the three elements into Great Space, Great Time, Great Knowledge and Ordinary Space, Ordinary Time and Ordinary Knowledge. The ordinary is what we humans occupy ourselves with in everyday life and the great relates to Infinity, Eternity, and Omniscience. The book is more than an exercise. It is a severe headache.

Whatever knowledge we want to download into Cogitator is up to us. If we want to regain control over the human ego, we can do so. If we want to remove the plutocracy, we can do that. This is an awesome responsibility.

Knowledge is Truth. Ordinary knowledge is the realm of ego and is tainted with all kinds of lies. There is only one evil on this planet and it is ego.

"Stubborn and ardent clinging to one's opinion is the best proof of stupidity."

— Michel Eyquem de Montaigne

Of all the experiences we have had, when do we actually KNOW what is true and what is not. If knowledge is Truth, how can we aspire to know what Truth is? In his book, "The Archaeology of Knowledge," Michel Foucault proposes that all prior knowledge is inborn and encoded in the DNA sequence of the double helix. All learning is simply a "re-cognition" of external stimuli whose vibrations match those we contain when we are born. We are a bundle of knowledge seeking our mirror images. Truth, in that context, is harmonization of our existence with what the universe REALLY is. This innate knowledge is instinct and resembles the operating system of a computer. What we "learn" is what was always within us. We "dis-cover" lies to find Truth. Like peeling an onion. What creates the human onion peels is the indoctrination and programming of cultures, politics, religions and the like. To find our true nature, we have to shed the mortal coils of incomplete knowledge.

The only foes that threaten America are the enemies at home, and these are ignorance, superstition, and incompetence.

Elbert Hubbard

Goals and Processes

"In the absence of clearly-defined goals, we become strangely loyal to performing daily trivia until we ultimate become enslaved by it"

Robert Heinlein

"Restlessness is discontent--and discontent is the first necessity of progress. Show me a thoroughly satisfied man and I will show you a failure."

— *Thomas Alva Edison*

The human ego body needs to maintain itself. This includes food, air, water and keeping itself in balance to maintain health. We have appetites. The basic needs have to be addressed before we can think of expanding our ego minds. If we have enough time to spend on development, we have choices. The priorities we set after we feel no threat are arbitrary. There is a cute story that illustrates setting priorities.

A professor stood before his Philosophy 101 class and had some items in front of him. When the class began, he wordlessly picked up a very large and empty mayonnaise jar and proceeded to fill it to the brim with golf balls. He then asked the students if the jar was full. They agreed that it was. He then brought out a box of pebbles and poured them into the jar while shaking the jar gently until the pebbles filled the areas between the golf balls. Again, he asked the students if the jar was full. They all agreed it was. He then picked up a box of sand and poured it into the jar and shook it until the sand filled the jar to the top. Once more, he asked if the jar was full. Once more, he got a unanimous YES! Now, the professor produced two cans of beer from under the table and poured the contents into the jar until the liquid reached the brim. All the students laughed, and, when the laughter subsided, the professor began his lecture:

"I want you all to recognize that this jar represents your life. The golf balls are the important things- - your health, your family, your partner, your children, your friends, your passions - - things that, if everything else was lost, your life would still be full. The pebbles are the other things that matter like your house, your job, and your car. The sand is everything else - - the small stuff."

He continues:

"If you put the sand into the jar first, there will be no room for the pebbles and golf balls. The same applies to your life. If you spend all your time and energy on the small stuff, there will be no room for those things that are really important to you. Pay attention to the things that are critical to your happiness. Play with your children, get your medical checkups, take your partner out dancing, play another 18. There will be enough time to go to work, fix the disposal, or clean the house. Take care of the golf balls first - - the things that really matter. Set your priorities according to those things because the remainder is just sand."

One of the students raised her hand and asked what the beer represented. The professor smiled:

"I'm glad you asked. It means that, no matter how full your life may seem, there's always room for a couple for a couple of beers!

(The above passage was part of a tour at a beer plant in Monroe, Wisconsin.)

When we think about what we want in life, we envision a State of Being that differs from our current State of Being. We seek to activate ourselves towards some **There and Then** from our **Here and Now**. We do this to add value to our self-worth or to create a better self-image and to achieve Peace of Mind.

The concept of time in terms of past, present and future is artificial and erroneous, of course. There will never be any past or future. You have the moment and that is all you will ever have. Whatever you create for yourself will be in the moment, this moment, and this is the moment that contains all moments. You are manipulated by calendars and schedules, but only because you accept it. Calendars were created by the plutocracy to make people do their bidding when they wanted it done. The truth is that **eternity IS the moment**. You can live forever in this moment.

All of us have time consciousness, some more than others. As Eckhart Tolle aptly describes in: "The Power of Now," eternity is Now. There is no other time. We only project from our mind what we call yesterday and tomorrow. We already live in eternity. Can this thought be conveyed any more elegantly? Learn more at www.eckharttolle.com.

The concept of space is also skewed for most people. There is no "there," only here. Here is a *point*. A point has no dimension. It is Infinity. You can project your universe into infinity from your Point of View. The only thing you will ever "see" is your own Mindscape from your point of view. You are able to create any element in your space because you have eternity to do it. This concept is the concept of Buddhahood and Christhood. You are totally responsible for what you create in your mindscape. Your ignorance is depicted in that space by anything your ego resents. The reason it is there and causing you discomfort is because you did not know what you were doing. You are your own Creator. You just never realized it before.

If you have trouble grasping this idea of your own Mindscape, start thinking about Niagara Falls and close your eyes. You can still picture it, right? How is that possible if it is not in your mind? Your eyes only convey vibrations. What you place in your mind is your choice. It is ego that sets the values for those images and stops you from keeping a beautiful picture in there.

Self-worth is the basis for ego's value system. Those who have a poor sense of self-worth normally will not aspire for enlightenment. They are the whiners and complainers who have never looked inside themselves for answers and see others' success as a reason to feel like a failure. Those who are seeking more values will set and achieve goals regularly and, with each accomplishment, will get a feeling of satisfaction and increase in self-worth. One of the worst things that happens when people reach a certain level of success (normally financial security), they stop thinking. They become conservative. The goal I set that eventually designed Cogitator was not for that purpose. I set out on a journey to discover my own being and why I did the things I did. Cogitator was a by-product of that goal. There are many more benefits to goal setting than simply reaching them. The experience along the path can be enlightening all by itself.

Commitment is the key to achievement. Many people will set goals for themselves in a frivolous way and never really commit to reaching them. Like losing weight, for example. Others will accept goals that are actually someone else's (like their parents' or teachers' goals) and never understand why they can't please those people. It is critical that honesty is first and foremost in choosing goals. There are many ways of prioritizing onc's goals, but one effective one is to separate them in short, medium and long range. Short being six months, medium being two or three years and, finally, lifetime goals. If we keep revisiting this list as we progress through NOW, we will reach some, drop some and refine some until we are at peace with ourselves. The way this works in the mind is that virtually all activity of each day becomes productive and self-fulfilling because we become aware of our actions <u>as they relate to our goals</u>. How do we prioritize this list?

Highest value is survival goals. Those automatically jump to Number One spot without ever being on our wish list. If we are occupied in our daily activities and we suddenly feel a sharp pain in the chest, we will drop what we are working on and make a beeline for the emergency room. If we can make it, it will stay top priority for some time to come and all future activities will be filtered through this experience. Survival goals are tied to our physical well being. Our bodies have need for oxygen, carbon-based food and water to maintain health and to feed the plants that feed us. We must sleep or die, so we sleep. We have a sex drive to propagate the species that is now used for other reasons than propagating the species. These needs take up a lot of our time and, if not satisfied, will nag at us until they are. However, as we develop our spiritual understanding to the point where we KNOW there is no such thing as Death (except of our past,) all goals take on much different values.

Security goals have to do with our "daily bread." Regardless of how we earn a living, until we have disposable income, it is difficult to work on enlightenment. Paying the bills on time and having money left over at the end of the month produces leisure time that can be used to better ourselves. Many people would rather watch TV or go to some sport event to pass this leisure time. Some will spend that time reading, taking classes, conversing with friends or family, etc... Having financial security brings us to the doorstep of enlightenment, but will not carry us over the threshold.

When we make decisions about how to structure and sequence activities, we *analyze* the value of each to try to ensure our time is well spent. These decisions are based upon our value and belief systems. Each activity is a Goal in our "To Do List." According to Buddhist schools of thought, we can contain 87 goals in our ego at any one time. Some of you better get cracking on your list. These goals are prioritized according to time, place, circumstance AND *effort.*

Desired Goal Value
Minus Perceived Effort Value
Equals Net Goal Value

Effort value subtracts from the gross value of each goal and what actually gets prioritized is the NET value of Goal value minus Effort value. Bingo! We're ready to go. Let's go for Number One. We activate ourselves towards that goal with the full intention of reaching it. In the process of achieving it, we have to be ready for unforeseen circumstances that may prevent us from reaching the goal. Look out! We may have to learn something we did not know! That is how we experience everything in life. Each day we can return to our crib having learned something or having mindlessly activated ourselves in the ruts of others' schools of thought. (The definition of a rut is a grave with the ends kicked out.)

If you have a PC, you know about the icons on your desktop. Each of the symbols represents a process that has meaning for you, whether it is a game, an accounting system, a web site, etc. The zeros and ones you activate by clicking on any of them will execute a sequence that will deliver the end result to you when you interact with it. Each one of those icons gets clicked because you have a goal you want to achieve with that sequence. Every "How To" book on the shelves is an example of a written icon. Every recipe book contains written icons for the preparation of meals.

In "Think and Grow Rich," Napoleon Hill addresses goal setting and prioritization. One of the exercises is to write down your goals in three categories: short, medium and long-term. You cannot find any kind of self-help book that does not include goal setting. If Buddhists are correct in the maximum of 87, it may be time to identify those.

There is nothing better to help you control your life than to sit down and actually write down what you think you lack. You will find that, the higher your level of understanding, the fewer creature comforts you desire. If you take the additional step of assigning priority to this list, you will probably discover your real motivation. The best way to assign priority is to look at your list and decide: "if I had to give up one of these, which one would go?" Mark that one with the last number. Keep doing this until you are left with the most important one. Once finished, you will have performed an *internal sort* to give you a better idea of what to do.

"If you truly wish to have everything, all you have to do is desire nothing."

Author

This is exactly how Cogitator is installed. It uses heuristic selection, just like you do, to determine the next most important activity to execute. It is the user that sets the priorities and is able to change those priorities as conditions demand. In the business environment, these priorities are all well known and controllable. In your personal life, these choices are not so easily defined.

Today, most of the hoi polloi's priorities are indoctrinated into them. The plutocracy presents a smorgasbord of choices to placate the rebellious mind. Like moths drawn to a flame, people imitate the activities of others in order to feel like part of the herd. In those 87 goals are all kinds of nonsensical doings. Television hypnotizes to the degree that few people would ever be able to occupy their day without it. The one-eyed beast captivates minds and makes them do whatever it wants. There is much activity that leads nowhere and provides huge incomes to the creators of that activity.

The ultimate goal is Peace of Mind. What provides this goal? - the knowledge that death is the opposite of birth and life never ends. How can you have peace of mind with all the stimuli you are bombarded with every day? - by retreating within your mindscape and uncreating them.

When you commit to achieving a goal, you have created a problem. A problem can be defined as the difference between what you think you are compared to what you think you want to be. You can define it the same way when you desire some material thing. If you have no goals, you have no problems. In this state of mind, get yourself a robe and go sit on the side of a mountain. In Buddhist thought, this is an arhat – one who has achieved nirvana and needs nothing and no one.

Many egos will make a basic mistake when choosing goals. They will *perceive a symptom as a problem.* This causes a lot of wasted effort. For example, if you have a headache and simply take aspirin for it, you may overlook a blocked artery that needs attention. For every manifestation to be addressed properly, you must eliminate the cause. Finding the cause is not easy, at times. The cause for all the strife on the planet is caused by the plutocracy, but how can you find out their identity? They certainly will not identify themselves.

Once you realize you create your own problems, there is no one else to blame for your state. The quality of life you have is defined by what you see within yourself. There are no needs.

Belief and Value

*"Those who can make you believe absurdities
can make you commit atrocities"*

Voltaire

Your ignorance is in your belief system. Your false beliefs and your false values prevent you from gaining understanding and harmony. There are so many layers of indoctrination and propaganda on the average mind that it is almost impossible to scrape them off the truth. You were not born ignorant. Ignorance is caused when you hide the truth you were born with. Values are also artificial. If the fabric of consciousness is all encompassing, how could any one element have any greater value than any other element?

If you've either seen or experienced something like a revival meeting, you may have seen and heard the leader of the group yelling at the crowd: "Do you believe?" Then, usually, the crowd will respond: "We believe!" *Translation: "Are you ignorant?" – "Yes, we are!"*

"They were so strong in their beliefs that there came a time when it hardly mattered what those beliefs were, they all fused into a single stubbornness"

Louise Erdrich

Belief and value are artificial constructs created by cultures, traditions and other institutions. They prevent progress because they are group egos and, like all egos, they will do anything to maintain an identity. More about this later but for the moment, think about what you did yesterday. What values did you gather during the day? Why did you choose those values over the infinite choices you had? Do you have a To Do List? Why are you placing those items on that list? What would happen to you if you did none of those items on the list?

Whatever makes sense matters. Whatever matters, makes sense. When we speak of the "material" world, we refer to the appearance of what "makes sense" to our ego. In our human form, we contain far more than flesh and bones, however. If we apply the principles of Quantum Mechanics to this thought, we will find that the particle is Matter and the wave makes Sense. It is this duality of being (the Eternal I/AM) that creates the consciousness we use to build our lives. It is the **Source of All Things** that Dr. Wayne Dyer (www.drwaynedyer.com) refers to in "The Power of Intention." It is the Force alluded to in "Star Wars." (*Incidentally, in "Stars Wars" there is no "Dark Side," merely the "Other Side" of the same coin.*) Just as Janus is depicted as two faces, Jekyll and Hyde as two alter egos, tragedy and comedy, etc., there is no possible way for the existence of any matter without the balancing factor of its opposite.

Opposite does not mean "bad." Opposite means what Newton implied when he said that "For every action, there is an equal and opposite reaction." What goes around comes around. It is only when ego makes value judgments that it can create pain for itself. Guilt is an illusion created by the plutocracy to enable it to manage the working class.

People get trained pretty well. I can remember some of the beliefs my mother used to try and inject me with. Everyone should trust his mom, right? Well, my mother was quite superstitious and terrified of thunderstorms. Many times she tried to transfer her fears into me, but to no avail. I was skeptical at a very early age. To give you some insight as to where my mind was when I was small, I remember lying on my back on the hill behind our house, looking up at a gorgeously starlit sky. It was the summer of 1950. I was five years old. The following thought came to mind: "It is the middle of the century. I wonder where I will be at the end of the century?" For a five year-old, this kind of thought is probably not common.

"The dissenter is every human being at those moments of his life when he resigns momentarily from the herd and thinks for himself."

— Archibald MacLeish

Regardless of what culture you were raised in and what value systems you were trained to adopt, you are the only one who can break through the veil of lies and misconceptions that society has heaped upon you. The fact of the matter is that the hoi polloi are there to serve the plutocracy and you can be sure the plutocracy will not be hasty in removing your ignorance. The nice thing is though, that you have contained the truth from day one. It has always been in you. All you have to do to *re*-cover it is to "*dis*-cover" it. That is, to remove all the false beliefs and indoctrination you have accepted as real. This is what happened to me and it can happen to you, as well.

After my experience, I did a number of things to try to understand what I had gone through. Reading hundreds of books was fine, but I still did not find one that said what I had felt. I still haven't. That's why I feel compelled to try and get this book out to you. There were a number of sources that came close, though. The best one is probably "Science and Health" by Mary Baker Eddy. You can read the book on-line at www.spirituality.com at your own pace. Another great help is "Time, Space and Knowledge" by Tartang Tulku. You can find out more about this fantastic view at www.dharmapublishing.com.

What seems to be a common element in the creation of ego is its need to feel grounded in some way. Egos have to have a touchstone to return to when it get confused. When Paul and I were discussing how Cogitator works, we continually had to give ourselves reality checks because we realized that mind is whatever we want it to be. Now, ten years after those discussions, I feel perfectly comfortable telling anyone that we can create whatever future we want. It's just that most people have no real idea of what it is they want.

I am convinced that a person's level of understanding relates to the size of his or her ego jar. There are many of the hoi polloi who cannot think in creative ways. It appears that, the larger the ego, the smaller the understanding.

Isms

"There is no instance of a country having benefited from prolonged warfare."

Sun-Tzu – The Art of War

Communism:
You have two cows. The government takes both,
milks them, keeps the milk, and gives you a pint.

Socialism:
The government takes one of your
cows and gives it to a neighbor.

Fascism:
The government takes both cows
and shoots one of them.

Nazism:
The government takes both cows and shoots you.

Capitalism:
You milk both cows, sell one of
the cows, and buy a bull.

Bureaucracy:
The government takes both cows, milks
them, and pours the milk down the drain.

Cultures will differ from continent to continent and country to country. When a scientist creates a culture in a laboratory, a growth medium (like agar) is introduced into a Petri dish and an organism is placed in it. As the organism feeds on the agar and multiplies, it creates a *culture* within its closed environment. This is the same concept as introducing a thought to a population and watching it grow. That is imperialism. A culture in society is a *school of thought.* Schools of thought are **isms**.

Indoctrination is the injection of a *school of thought* into an ego. When an ego adopts an ism as a real thing in its belief system, it is trapped. The most common ism the plutocracy uses is Imperialism. This is the introduction of an idea into a culture that eventually changes that culture to the plutocracy's "way of thinking."

"Faith and Belief are poor substitutes for Truth"

Author

Tradition and legends carry meanings and value systems from one generation to the next. They have served a purpose, but must be abandoned when greater knowledge proves their inaccuracy. Joseph Campbell had a clear picture of how these myths affect us as human beings. In all his works, he defines the common threads that weave our existence in a wonderful way. Much more can be found at www.jcf.org. He is a must read for those on the seeker path.

"The great enemy of the truth is very often not the lie—deliberate, contrived, and dishonest—but the myth—persistent, persuasive, and unrealistic."

John F. Kennedy

This world is filled with propaganda, disinformation and outright lies that have the ability to manipulate weak minds. (Politicians and advertisers are well aware of this.) If we do not seek more knowledge and understanding, how are we to determine what is true? According to Foucault, all knowledge is encoded in us at birth. How else could we breathe, cry, eat, purge, and sleep from the day we are born without having to go to class for it? How does an acorn know to become an oak tree and not a pine tree? If we indeed are encoded with all the Truth of all history, why are we willing to believe lies? The only Satan is the human ego. The first step on the path of enlightenment is to kill this worthless beast. We have to stop believing in imaginary garbage. Society and government officials are the problem, not their components. The laws established to maintain the plutocracy have to change.

"Violence is the tool of the ignorant"

Another effective ism for the plutocracy is patriotism. This ism is the cause of all wars because it creates the individual corrals in which various herds can be stored. Artificial borders are established to make people get passports and visas before they can cross these imaginary lines. When the plutocracy wants to make something happen, it stirs the ignorance of one herd or the other (usually both) to create conflict. Flag wavers are quite dangerous. Their ignorance is legend.

"He who joyfully marches to music rank and file has already earned my contempt. He has been given a large brain by mistake since, for him the spinal cord would surely suffice. This disgrace to civilization should be done away with at once. Heroism on command, how violently I hate all this, how despicable and ignoble war is; I would rather be torn to shreds than be part of so base an action. It is my conviction that killing under the cloak of war is nothing but an act of murder."

Albert Einstein

War is created by the plutocracy because of the desire for power. The military/industrial complex thrives on war. There is absolutely no question that war today is caused for economic control that translates into power. Plutocrats have no problem culling the herd for their own benefit. To end war, when someone gives you license to kill another human being, the first person to kill is the licensor.

Another reason for war is for the plutocracy to test their next generation of technological advances. Since it would be difficult to herd a bunch of people into ovens in this day and age, plutocrats will force "volunteers" to play the role of guinea pigs under the guise of "national security." How can you test the effectiveness of your next diabolical contraption without using it?

If you know about H. G. Wells' "The Time Machine," you may recall the separation of the races into Morlocks and Eloi. The Eloi are childlike and playful and spend their time frolicking and seemingly have not a care in their lives. The protagonist later finds out that there is an underground race of Morlocks who, when hungry, sound sirens to hypnotize the Eloi to file into an aboveground entrance. When enough Eloi have entered, the doors close and the sirens stop. Then, the Morlocks can sit down to dinner on nice, young, tender meat. In today's society, Morlocks represent the plutocracy and the hoi polloi are the Eloi. The only difference from the book is that the plutocracy feeds on minds, instead of bodies.

"The missionary located a primitive tribe of cannibals and settled into trying to convert them to Western ways and thought and behavior. He spent many evenings around the fire conversing with the cannibal chieftain, who was considered quite a sage and reminisced at length about his many victorious campaigns and all the people he had eaten in the process.

"Ah, but our wars are fought for a higher purpose," expounded the missionary. "For religious freedom, for democracy, for truth..."

The cannibal nodded, "You must eat many, many people," he commented admiringly.

"Oh no!" The missionary was shocked. "We don't eat humans."

"Then," the chieftain pointed out, "you have no reason to kill each other.""

The ignorance of patriots can only be matched by the ignorance of the religious. The borders these fools create are not only imaginary, but also intangible. Can you imagine someone saying that they believe in some "god" and yet be willing to go to war? The only thing religion creates is a hypocrite. How can anyone say that "god" is omniscient, omnipresent and omnipotent and not see "god" in all people and all things? Take your Bible, your Quran, your Torah and whatever else you quote from and shove them where the sun doesn't shine. Ego jars for the bible thumpers are very small and very thick. If there were really a God in the sense that most believe in Him, we would have been eliminated long ago. We are not created to be any Being's toys. We project Him to be like our own image, but that is simply anthropomorphism on our part.

"Religion was invented by the rich to keep them from being killed by the poor."

Bumper Sticker seen in Chicago

Power is bestowed to those who are "in the know." When you start thinking about what purpose we serve on this planet, what comes to your mind? In the Maslow pyramid, the social level actually is where Social Stratification takes place. The plutocracy wants to be at the top of all human activity. The pyramid, of course, is very symbolic. If you look at the Great Seal of the United States on the back of the dollar bill, you will see another pyramid. This is the obverse side of the Great Seal and has not been seen very often. It has twelve levels with the all-seeing eye of Divine Providence at its peak. In Buddhism, there are also twelve levels of enlightenment. If you were to stratify the population according to its levels of enlightenment, the pyramid could be a relatively accurate depiction with the majority of human egos not having a clue of what level they live in. The term *Annuit Coeptis* above the pyramid translates to something like: "He has smiled on our undertakings." Underneath the pyramid, *Novus Ordo Seclorum* translates to: "New Order of the Ages."

The dollar bill has allowed consumerism to run rampant. People *consume* the earth. Every large concentration of egos is like a cancer on the skin of the planet. This ism is what is causing destruction of the Balance of Nature.

No matter what you may call yourself, as soon as you identify what you stand for, you expose your isms. All isms are false to some degree. Belief systems like Capitalism, Communism, Judaism, Existentialism, Monism, Dualism, Pluralism, ad infinitum are all partially true, but not the final Truth. They are simply schools of thought. The most important goal for any human ego is Peace of Mind. The only way to find it is to understand Truth and the only place you will find truth is within yourself.

"The truth shall set you free."

The ruling ism today is imperialism. This works the same way as a laboratory culture, but introduces ideas rather than organisms into a "Petri country" to see how it grows. Plutocrats use propaganda and many forms of lies and misinformation to sway public opinion. Power and influence are meted out to various parts of the globe based upon controlling each segment of the population. If the plutocracy needs to move its influence faster, it starts a war.

The following lyrics from Eagles' Brian Wilson illustrate the point:

The Last Resort

She came from Providence,
The one in Rhode Island
Where the old world shadows hang heavy in the air
She packed her hopes and dreams
Like a refugee
Just as her father came across the sea

She heard about a place people were smilin'
They spoke about the red man's way,
And how they loved the land
And they came from everywhere
To the Great Divide
Seeking a place to stand
Or a place to hide

Down in the crowded bars
Out for a good time,
Can't wait to tell you all,
What it's like up there
And they called it Paradise
I don't know why
Somebody laid the mountains low
While the town got high

Then the chilly winds blew down
Across the desert
Through the canyons of the coast, to the Malibu
Where the pretty people play hungry for power
To light their neon way
And give them things to do

Some rich men came and raped the land
Nobody caught 'em
Put up a bunch of ugly boxes and Jesus,
People bought 'em
And they called it paradise
The place to be

They watched the hazy sun, sinking in the sea

You can leave it all behind
And sail to Lahaina
Just like the missionaries did, so many years ago
They even brought a neon sign "Jesus is coming"
Brought the white man's burden down
Brought the white man's reign

Who will provide the grand design?
What is yours and what is mine?
'Cause there is no more new frontier
We have got to make it here

We satisfy our endless needs and
Justify our bloody deeds,
In the name of destiny and the name of God

And you can see them there
On Sunday morning
They stand and sing about what it's like up there
They call it paradise
I don't know why
You call someplace paradise
Kiss it goodbye

Because of a basic human desire to socialize, isms serve the purpose of creating clubs, groups, countries, religions and the like. These factions cause wars and strife by comparing one ism against another ism and announcing that their misbelief is better than another group's misbelief. This keeps people busy and off the neck of the plutocracy.

"Success, recognition, and conformity are the bywords of the modern world where everyone seems to crave the anesthetizing security of being identified with the majority."

— *Martin Luther King, Jr.*

Control over individuals and groups by the plutocrats is exercised by creating the concept of competition. Business, sports and ego displays are for the purpose of "winning." Divide and conquer is the objective. Egos feel the need to "take sides" and miss the fact that there are no sides.

Conscience is an artificial construct that gets indoctrinated into most children as soon as possible. Original sin, my ass. *Con* means against and *science* means knowledge. Conscience goes against what is true. The plutocrats use the ignorance of their subjects to make them work for their own benefit by forcing conscience into them. The truth is that **everyone is always doing the very best they can under the circumstances**. The only circumstances of every situation are time, space and knowledge.

"America is the only country that went from barbarism to decadence without civilization in between"

Oscar Wilde

The hoi polloi need distractions to keep them busy, so the plutocrats create **busi**-*ness*. They create crime, so that we may play cops and robbers, they present gratuitous violence like football and ultimate fighting to redirect our anger, they build amusement parks for us to waste time and money. The reason for plutocrats to censor the truth is to keep the herds ignorant of what it is doing and to provide distractions that prevent rebellion. Rather than paying attention to global warming and destruction of animals and habitats, people will look forward to the Super Bowl. Especially in the United States, there are so many distractions for people to have "fun" rather than achieve peace and joy, it borders on the ridiculous. Keep people ignorant and have them spend their money on nonsense. That's the American Way. P. T. Barnum was right when he said: "There's no underestimating the intelligence of the American public."

The weakness of egos participating in nonsensical activities is what creates the consumer society. The mindless spending of time and money by the ignorant is what keeps the plutocrats in charge.

There are so many misconceptions, misunderstand-
ings, and downright ignorance in the human population that it really is difficult to grab a hold of the truth.
A lot of this has to do with language and other ways
of communicating. Television is the biggest hypnotist,
followed by other media that intentionally depict what
they need to depict to maintain balance for the plutocracy. Lies upon lies and the herd follows like lemmings
to the ocean.

**"Propaganda is the art of persuading others
of what you don't believe yourself."**

— Abba Eban

Truth is not determined by majority vote. It doesn't
reside in words or rhetoric, belief or faith, or any ism.
You must adopt a philosophy for you to live your life
as you wish. You can achieve whatever you want, not
necessarily by learning something new, but by scraping
away all the lies you have muddling up your thoughts.
Truth has always been within you. It is just buried under the compost heap of society. Surviving until you die
is not the way to pass through this life, unless you wish
to remain ignorant. It is absolutely fruitless for you to
look outside yourself for answers. Even as you read
these words, you may be starting to realize that they
were always within you. They are stated in a sense you
never considered before, perhaps. You may be taking
a different Point of View, but the view was always there

for you to see. All you need to do to see a different Point of View is to change your attitude.

Breaking through the veil of lies is not easy after the indoctrination has taken hold. Ego is based upon false beliefs. It creates a "mind of its own" soon after birth. It develops from the baby stage by attaching values of what "feels good" and what "feels bad" as it encounters life. The animal instinct is strong as with all animals and this instinct is what the plutocracy uses to manage the herd. After indoctrination has taken hold, the next thing that controls people is Force of Habit.

The way habits get ingrained in memory is when our neural networks are fired by repetition. If you take a certain route to a grocery store or to work, you will sometimes find it difficult to explore different ways of getting there. If you are accustomed to lighting a cigarette after dinner, you will have difficulty when restaurants go smokeless. Habits resemble ruts. The deeper the rut, the more difficult it is to change direction. If habits control your life, you are already dead. The definition of a rut is: a coffin with the ends kicked out. Habits are the same as addictions when executed without thought.

Habits are based upon seeking a certain goal. For example, many people will make it a habit to go to church on Sunday. Mostly, whatever they get from it is based on their observation of what others seem to get from that activity. It may actually be for spiritual fulfillment or just to socialize. Very few people will ever think about the fact that "Sunday" is an arbitrary name given to one of seven days is a week. Since the only time we ever exist is the Now, the entire calendar is illusory and arbitrary. Why should one day be more important than another? Why don't we change the calendar to twelve months of thirty days each and leave the extra days of the solar year as World Peace days?

We can play all kinds of games with this calendar concept. It exists primarily so that people can do busyness in specific time frames. Why do we have holidays? This is just another distraction to make the herds look forward to having fun. It's also another reason to take your hard-earned money and spend it on nonsense. Most holidays are appeals to emotion. Why do we need an excuse to feel good? Treat every day as containing all holidays and don't be conned by the plutocrats.

Why don't we have forty weeks of nine days each and have people work three days on – three days off. This way each job could have two employees and everyone could work. The stress release would be fantastic. Many other ways of passing life could be imagined. If you find it difficult to picture these new concepts, you have a thick ego jar.

Almost all adult activities are performed by the Force of Habit. Whereas the Spirit Force serves as the fulfilling force in life, ego Force chooses goals to make it stronger and feel better. Those goals are achieved through a sequence of related thoughts and actions that create memories. When the neural networks that achieve the goal are fired, the thoughts and actions are "re-membered" when the goal has to be achieved again. The more often you repeat the action, the stronger the habit becomes. Constant repetition of the same action soon makes it become a "mind-less" routine that is activated by stimulus. This is what is used to "train" people into doing routines that achieve specific goals. The first step in changing your life is to become aware of these "Trains of Thought."

Trains of thought are *re-membered* very much like the activities of a railroad yard. When a locomotive going to Chicago is linked to boxcars in Los Angeles, there is a plan for its route and the various stops it can make along the route. For example, Denver and Kansas City may have some boxcars going to Chicago, so the locomotive will enter their train yards to drop some boxcars off and pick some up. Each boxcar (member) has a destination to fulfill for each train run. This is how you gather your previous experiences to achieve your destination(s). Once the route is learned, more complex combinations of trains of thought can be re-membered for more efficient and effective delivery of goals. That is how we learn.

Another analogy for gathering thought is to imagine a river. Every river has a source and finds its way to its end. The source can be compared to the birth of a thought and, as the thought flows, it gathers size and strength during its travels. It will always take the path of least resistance. Nothing can stop the flow until it reaches a larger body of water. The only thing that changes during its course is its name. What truly happens though, is that the river is just part of the water cycle. One of its water molecules today may have been in a different river some time prior. In fact, you can be certain that it was. Just because we name a specific stream doesn't change the fact that all streams are part of the same system. It is the same thing for our thoughts. Each and every thought is connected to every other thought, just like a water molecule is connected to the water cycle. Egos just go to war over what to name those thoughts.

Cogitator has no habits. It will always take the path of least resistance to accomplishing what it is supposed to do. We humans actually do the same, but our emotions will interfere with the path and make it more difficult than it needs to be. It is said that we have will power, but the truth is ego only has "won't power." The real you always knows the best way of achieving but ego gets to say yea or nay to the best choice. Your feelings always tell you the truth, but your ego judges regardless. It thinks it's smart. It is always ignorant.

A habit is just a routine or program that always gets activated based on a stimulus. These are injected into your mind by "training." If you ever accepted a new job, you know that part of your orientation is to be "trained." Trains of thought will be given to you to absorb your new company's "way of doing things." The stimulus may be visual, verbal, a smell or a touch, but it reacts the same way as when you click on an icon on your PC. When you are "clicked," you perform whatever routine that particular icon represents. It may be brushing your teeth, taking a shower, driving to work, whatever...

Robots are becoming more and more prevalent. It is only a matter of time until the physical movements of human beings can be replicated in a machine. Right now, much of the population behaves as robots do, but they still have feelings that get in the way of predictability. Robots will not talk or balk at their assigned duties. The plutocracy programs people to do what it wants them to do, but robots will be much easier to control and they will not ask for money, either. The hoi polloi will soon be superfluous in the mind of the plutocracy. It may soon be time to cull the herd. There's another reason for getting rid of excess people - they have to eat.

Have you ever considered how much waste of energy, money, time and food is created by today's generation? What is being accomplished other than make the rich richer? Lots of people are having fun and playing all kinds of games. Entertainment is big industry. The really important things in life are ignored because: *"I just can't find the time...*" The consumer consumes and consumes and consumes based on habit. Soon, the earth will be consumed unless the madness can be stopped.

Staying ignorant will not improve any situation. All you have to do to change the world is to change your mind. The only way to change your mind is to unlearn what you believe and start recognizing truth.

"Divine metaphysics, as revealed to spiritual understanding, shows clearly that all is Mind, and that Mind is God, omnipotence, omnipresence, omniscience, -- that is, all power, all presence, all Science. Hence all is in reality the manifestation of Mind."

From Science and Health by Mary Baker Eddy

All religionisms are cases of arrested development. They confine their members and prevent their individual spiritual growth by creating the idea of guilt. It is when people are willing to accept faith and belief as substitutes for truth that they become pawns in the hands of the chess players. They are the fleas in the flea circus. The truth will indeed set you free, but until then you are subjected to being a pawn.

"Nothing is real and eternal, - nothing is Spirit, - but God and His idea. Evil has no reality, it is neither person, place, nor thing, but is simply a belief, an illusion of material sense"

From Science and Healthby Mary Baker Eddy

Spirituality goes beyond the childish teachings of many religions. It is the understanding that the fabric of consciousness IS God. We are part of that fabric and there is no possible way for us to separate ourselves from any of it. Ego wants to blame others for the condition is observes, not knowing the illusion and pain was created by itself. Ego strives to place values on life and its experiences, but it cannot ever command life in its efforts. Mastery of Life as taught by the Rosicrucians is, very simply, to enjoy every aspect of it. This is also the same idea the Buddha was conveying, Jesus was conveying, Lord Krishna was conveying to Arjuna in the Baghavad Gita, and every intelligent being conveys. Guilt was created by the plutocracy to control the herd. Use it whichever way you want. There is no such thing as sin or guilt in the Kingdom of God, only in the puny human ego.

"For certain is death for the born and certain is birth for the dead; therefore over the inevitable thou shalt not grieve."

— Bhagavad Gita 2:27

When we speak of the "material" world, we refer to the appearance of what "makes sense" to our ego. This is materialism. In our human form, we contain far more than flesh and bones, however. The duality of being (the Eternal I/AM) that creates the consciousness we use is how we build our lives. It is the **Source of All Things** that Dr. Wayne Dyer (www.drwaynedyer.com) refers to in "The Power of Intention" and the Force alluded to in "Star Wars." Incidentally, in "Stars Wars" there is no "Dark Side," merely the "Other Side" of the same coin. Just as Janus is depicted as two faces, Jekyll and Hyde as two alter egos, tragedy and comedy, etc., there is no possible way for existence of any matter without the balancing factor of its opposite.

Opposite does not mean "bad." Opposite means what Newton implied when he said that "For every action, there is an equal and opposite reaction." What goes around comes around. It is only when ego makes value judgments that it can create pain for itself. Guilt is an illusion created by the plutocracy to enable them to manage the working class.

People get trained pretty well. I can remember some of the beliefs my mother used to try and inject me with. Everyone should trust his mom, right? Well, my mother was quite superstitious and terrified of thunderstorms. Many times she tried to transfer her fears into me, but to no avail. I was skeptical at a very early age. To give you some insight as to where my mind was when I was small, I remember lying on my back on the hill behind our house, looking up at a gorgeously starlit sky. It was the summer of 1950. I was five years old. The following thought came to mind: "It is the middle of the century. I wonder where I will be at the end of the century?" For a five year-old, this kind of thought is probably not common.

"The dissenter is every human being at those moments of his life when he resigns momentarily from the herd and thinks for himself."

— Archibald MacLeish

The "System"

"In politics there is no honor."
— Benjamin Disraeli

When I started doing systems analysis, I didn't have the foggiest notion of how systems are all interconnected. As I gathered more experience, it became clear that the inputs for one system were the outputs of other systems and that every output from any system invariably would be input for yet more systems. When Paul and I were discussing how Cogitator could be used in business, we knew that every business contained the same functions and the same goals. We had seen data processing morph into information processing, then rule-based systems, then knowledge management and finally, into today's intelligent systems.

This evolution has resulted in a tremendously complex structure based upon method-based software. Paul and I saw the solution to the complex environment as the separation of data (facts), function (instruction), context and goals. The problem of programming is not the creation of a routine that satisfies a particular transaction. The problem arises when there is a change of value(s) within a system. Program maintenance is the most costly activity on the planet. An additional problem arises when maintenance is not done or is done incorrectly. With Cogitator, there is no program maintenance. Because the elements are individually gathered to service a transaction, only the changing element needs to be changed.

Compare this concept with a recipe for a favorite dish. If you follow a recipe to the letter as depicted in your recipe file, you will probably end up with a decent meal. However, if you want to get creative and use a sprig of parsley in the mixture, you will add your personal touch to the goal. In traditional programming, you would have to find the program for that recipe, insert "add sprig of parsley" to the instructions, reassemble the program for execution and you could have your new recipe the next time the program was run. With Cogitator, you go to the ingredient list and place "add sprig of parsley" in it at the appropriate step. That's it.

A recipe in Cogitator is called a scenario. The user with the use of elements, functions, qualifications, context and goals creates scenarios. All are independent and interdependent. As more and more scenarios are loaded into the knowledge base Cogitator uses, it gains "experience." With each interaction with users, it "learns."

The Big Picture depicts the relationship of all subsidiary systems to "THE SYSTEM." If you want to see the Big Picture, you have to break your ego jar. Until the Grand Unification Theory is published, we will have to deal with words and symbols to try and describe this picture. In the United States and most of the Western World, the System is the economic system. The big picture shows how money is used to manage the population. Business, Politics, and Religion work together to maintain control of The System. The plutocracy sets the rules for all these systems because the eventual result is the control of the flow of money. Control the flow of money and you control people who use money.

Business systems all have the same goal - Profit. They must keep Balance in Assets and Liabilities (Balance Sheet) while activating their resources to do productive work (Income Statement.) Debits and Credits are applied against the general ledger to add and subtract money from the balance sheet to determine whether or not the operation of the business is profitable. In this finite universe, emotion does not exist. It is the perfect environment for an Artificial Mind that considers results as they relate to financial goals in its decision-making. All systems work this exact same way. They just have different inputs and outputs.

Money is one of the best motivators for the plutocracy to use to control people. If people feel they need money to survive, you can bet everyone has his price. It doesn't really matter to the plutocrats how much money they have to pass around because they know how to always get it back.

Political systems set policies. These are rules for the operation of businesses and civilized conduct. They are normally contained in a *constitution.* Different countries will operate on various constitutions that the leadership is supposed to monitor. Laws are enacted to prevent too much variation from the constitutional state. There are no democracies, republics, or any other type of politics. There is only the plutocracy.

What's the difference between baseball and politics?
— In baseball you're out if you're caught stealing.

Religious systems create conscience. "Con" means against and "Science" means knowledge, therefore the conscience religions try to have you swallow is against knowledge. They use your ignorance to make you believe that, if policies and laws are violated, you will be punished. There is no spirituality in organized religion. It's all dogmatic crap.

Business creates material desires and Religion creates spiritual desires.

The only thing that institutional systems create is a hypocrite. The only way to dissolve institutions that take advantage of ignorance is to gain knowledge. It's on you. If you are not willing to break free of your jar, you are part of the problem. The solution is knowledge.

Most of my experience in the computer world came from dealing with large corporations, primarily the Fortune 1000. Initially, programming for LaSalle National Bank gave me insight as to how money is managed and how banks create money. When I returned to the bank after Vietnam and college, I was assigned to evaluate how other banks around the country were using current technology. I traveled with a bank officer to meet with major banks and try to understand how their methods may be beneficial to the development of LaSalle.

Rather than having this sound like a resume, I will try to depict some of what I learned in over thirty years in this business.

> ➤ At Eureka Williams in Bloomington, Illinois, I worked on a Bill of Material application that taught me how components create an end product. It wasn't until much later that I realized that our DNA is the Bill of Material for us. The knowledge of how the pieces are assembled is the same as the memes in our DNA.
> ➤ At University Computing Company from Dallas, Texas, I sold software that enhanced the capability of Operating Systems. I also was the national representative assigned to sell the IMS Data Dictionary. Experience with major companies like John Deere, Blue Cross/Blue Shield and the like taught me how information was used and managed by large corporations. When UCC developed UCC 7, a computer center scheduling system, I learned that all application systems are connected to the Operating System and can be controlled by a central function.

> ➢ At List Processing Company (LPC) I learned how the Zip + 4 code in the mailing address is tied to the census demographics. Your neighborhood is rated and graded, based on economic and ethnic data. The messages you get in your mailbox are very much "smart" messages.
> ➢ At Unitech Systems, I sold a balancing system that would eliminate the need for humans to check totals at the end of a process. Knowing that one process' output creates the input for one or more systems solidified the fact that all systems are interconnected and automation will replace any human function involving a decision.
> ➢ While designing a supply chain management proposal for W. W. Grainger, I realized that information from the point of sale all the way back to the source of Raw Materials could be tracked and managed.

All the elements listed above are candidates for knowledge bases. Manufacturing processes, shipping schedules, money transfers, virtually all elements of human activity can be stored and accessed on knowledge bases. If Cogitator can be made aware of this knowledge and how the flow is to be controlled, who needs management?

"The System" is a socialization system. Whenever power was doled out to the members of the plutocracy, it was forever surrendered. We live according to the way they dictate. The games they play are on a global basis and the rules are much different than those they enforce on the hoi polloi. With technology advances, the plutocracy now uses robotic systems to monitor the population. There are "smart" traffic signals to allow an easier flow of traffic, cameras that can have a citation sent to your home if you ignore a stop sign, transponders that record what toll way you used, (and when.) Surveillance systems are everywhere around. The place we really need these things is in the offices of the plutocracy.

Business, politics and religion are all in cahoots. They use the very same tactics to manipulate weak minds. They all use ignorance to move the emotions of their members. Emotion is the only thing they need to make the herds move where they want. Human egos are the only creatures that can laugh or cry and these two motivators are constantly in use by the plutocrats. Human egos also are the only creatures that kill for purposes other than to feed. When is this madness going to end?

Wisdom

"Honesty is the first chapter of the book of wisdom."

- Thomas Jefferson

"Wisdom is greater than knowledge, for wisdom includes knowledge and the due use of it."

Joseph Burritt Sevelli Capponi

The **Thought Process of Becoming** is what you must become aware of if you want to improve your life and get on the road to enlightenment. The only way you will create heaven for yourself is to change your mind. The only thing you have to change in your mind in order to come to be is to stop thinking about anything else. Take a stand in your Point of View, live in the moment, (there is no past or future) and project yourself as the angel you really are.

"He who knows not, and knows not that
he knows not, is a fool; shun him.
He who knows not, and knows that he
knows not, is a student; teach him.
He who knows, and knows not that
he knows, is asleep; wake him.
He who knows, and knows that he
knows, is wise; follow him."

— Asian proverb

Your Process of Becoming is determined by what you think you want (goal,) what you think you understand (knowledge) and what circumstances you think you face at the moment. When you feel "out of balance," you try to orient yourself, take stock of the circumstances that surround you, and make a decision about the action that you must take to regain your balancc. Then, you prioritize this action on your To Do List, whether in your mind or on a piece of paper and you either go to the next itch to scratch or begin acting upon your first priority. One major point to understand here: **You are ALWAYS acting upon your number one priority.**

For you to change your life to a higher plane, you must review those activities you perform (and have performed) and reevaluate why you do what you do and why you did what you did. The most difficult thing to do in self-evaluation is to evaluate what you feel about your State of Being and how you got there. If you have been in your Comfort Zone for a while, you may have become complacent about developing further. After all, if you have no bills and a hefty financial backing, what could prompt you to do anything different than what you always have done? You can now prepare yourself for death and you may already have picked your final "resting place." If that is the case, then you are already dead.

The most important realization you need to make here is that you never "see" anything except in your own mind. The "out there" is the vision you project after you process the sensory input you could interpret. "Out There" is **your** output. Therein lie the keys to freedom. If you want to improve your State of Being, you must learn to interpret more of the information your senses send to your mind. You must gain more knowledge and understanding. The Time, Place, and Knowledge trinity of circumstances need to be understood for what they really are.

Knowledge

"Knowledge is the only fountain both of the love and the principles of human liberty."

- William Wordsworth.

You are taught from an early age to recognize, categorize, prioritize and sort into sequence whatever stimuli you can sense. These activities make you decide what to do next. Most educational systems in industrialized countries will teach elements that will make an individual useful in society, rather than elements of self-realization. For you to enlighten yourself, you have to desire it and make it a goal. You will never be able to know anyone else better than you know yourself. The first element to know on the road to enlightenment is you.

"Self examination is the key to insight, which is the key to wisdom."

M. Scott Peck – Meditation from the Road.

Awareness

The fool can no more taste the sweet-ness of wisdom than the man with a cold can appreciate the scent of a rose.

— North African saying

Awareness is your ability to recognize vibratory stimuli that harmonize with your own composition. It is the knowledge you contain. You "tune in" by reflecting the stimuli against your mind (common sense) until you can identify what the stimuli are. You "re-cognize" what you can understand from the knowledge you already contain. As a baby, you had no restrictions on being what you are. It is only later that you were taught things that are not natural. This is when you begin to develop an **Identity**. This identity is your ego structure and is the thing you need to examine to get control of your life. Becoming aware of your ego necessitates a conscious, realistic, truthful, and objective awareness of your thoughts, feelings, and attitudes. You must ask yourself why you think what you think, why you feel what you feel and why you do what you do. You must learn how you create your reality.

Take a common example like going to the grocery store. You look in your refrigerator and see the butter tray empty, so you take a pencil and look for your grocery list to add it on. You look around a bit more in the pantry and the rest of the refrigerator to add more items before preparing to shop for food. You check yourself to see if you are presentable, get the car keys, drive out of your garage to proceed to your local store and return home with your bags of groceries. You start putting things away in their normal storage spot and come upon the butter you bought and place a stick in the tray. You achieved the goal you had envisioned when you noticed the empty tray. What just happened?

All the functions you performed to get that stick of butter in the tray were goals being visualized and achieved by Processes of Becoming executed in the proper sequence. They were all achieved by the concepts of Time, Place, Knowledge, and circumstances. You probably were not even aware that the routines were being executed as you went through the entire process. The detail involved in what you just accomplished is nothing short of awesome, however. There are so many things we all take for granted about our daily life that we miss what living is about.

When you saw the empty tray, you felt a need. According to Maslow's hierarchy of needs, this would fall at the bottom of the pyramid at the survival level. You began taking inventory of your circumstances when you realized butter was an issue. You imagined where you were (place) and when it was (time) to make a decision about getting more butter. You began going through a mental checklist to analyze and evaluate whether or not going to the store was the next proper action to take. Because you have company coming for dinner, you decide to make this the next priority of your day. You commit. You now consult your knowledge base for the information you need to place that stick of butter in its tray. You want to change your State of Being from one that has no butter to the State of Being that has that stick of butter in the tray.

Your thoughts now begin to gather the Process of Becoming someone with butter. As you get ready for the trip, you gather the items you need to make it successful. You need keys, wallet with credit cards, clothes on your body appropriate for the weather, etc. Inventory complete, you begin to expend energy to move your body. As the calories from your nourishment start burning, the mass begins to move towards the direction of the garage. Directly in front of you, your mind interprets the electromagnetic spectrum vibrations on your eyes' rods and cones as a wall, so you turn your path to avoid it, opting for what you interpret as an opening in that wall. Negotiating your way through your house in that same manner, you head towards what your ego tells you is the garage door.

At the door, you notice a round protrusion about hand-high that you call a doorknob. Knowing its function, you grasp it, turn it and push the door forward. Closing the garage door behind you, you activate the "Open Car Door" routine, "Sit in Driver Seat" routine, "Fasten Seat Belt" routine, "Place Car Key in Ignition Slot" routine, "press Garage Door Opener Button" routine, "Put Foot on Brake" routine, "Turn Ignition Key" routine, "Engage Transmission" routine, "Lift Foot from Brake Pedal" routine, and let the engine expend energy through the explosions of gasoline so that the pistons can force the wheels to turn. You are changing your Place.

You are now in your "Drive to the Grocery Store" routine. You notice that the gas gauge is nearing one-fourth full, so you check your circumstances again. Location, time and knowledge make you alter your route to activate your "Fill Gas Tank" routine. After the tank is full, you resume your "Drive to Grocery Store" routine from a different perspective.

Here, your societal learning makes you aware of traffic signals, stop signs, lane markings, and the like. As you reach the store, you activate your "Look for Parking Spot" routine. Finding an appropriate spot, you activate the "Slow and Enter Parking Space" routine, "Brake When Fully in Space" routine, "Disengage Transmission and Place in Park" routine, "Turn Ignition Key Off and Remove" routine, "Grasp and Pull Car Door Release Lever" routine, "Push Door Open" routine, and "Step Out of The Car" routine.

As you step out of the car, your inner ear gives you the feeling of balance that you need and you place one foot in front of the other without falling and you reach the entryway. Activate "Grocery shopping" routine. Check your list, plan your path through the aisles and look for sale items. Your preprogrammed routines will continue to execute in sequence until the butter is in the tray. So what?

The above example is how you conduct your life for every single goal you imagine. You use your innate knowledge with your learned knowledge to achieve any goal you consider important. There is much more detail involved with the above scenario, but that will wait. Just as long as you understand this is the only way every human being functions. Your learned knowledge is what differentiates you from natural life. Acorns don't need butter.

If you are like most people, virtually every day is structured in such a way that you have very little original thinking to do. The routines you have internalized over time simply get activated whenever you feel the need. You do things "because you've always done it that way." Your Comfort Zone has been established and you know how to stay in homeostatic balance. When are you going to wake up and seek what all people really want? Are you just going to wait for the advertisers to motivate you with some new stimulus for you to send them more money? How long will you let others hypnotize you into supporting their goals? You must learn to think "outside the envelope."

"What you are, so is your world. Everything in the universe is resolved into your own inward experience. It matters little what is without, for it is all a reflection of your own state of consciousness. It matters everything what you are within, for everything without will be mirrored and colored accordingly."

– Path to Prosperity

You accept much of what you do because you were programmed by society. The values you assign to the various stimuli you process are not real. If you ever saw a travelogue where schools of fish are scared by a predator, you see that they all respond at the same moment in changing direction. So it is with the human herd after the programming is finished. You must deprogram the bunk to improve yourself. No one will do it for you.

"A man's weakness and strength, purity and impurity, are his own and not another man's. They are brought about by himself and not by another; and they can only be altered by himself, never by another. His condition is also his own, and not another man's. His sufferings and his happiness are evolved from within."

-From "As A Man Thinketh" by James Allen

There is only one Mind. Egos try to create a "mind of their own" and are normally in conflict with the balance of nature. It is a futile exercise. When you harmonize your ego to make it in concert with the Universal Mind, you have mastered your life forever. You are totally responsible for what you are and what you feel. You must reprogram yourself to achieve this. You have to take the stance that there is nowhere else to find truth in all its glory, save to imagine, meditate and contemplate your actions. You have to live with the pursuit of a philosophy to express your being. "Philosophy" means "love of knowledge," or "love of wisdom" and the acquisition of those elements will erase all misinformation that causes you pain. You must begin to find your true self if you want your life to get better.

Imagine for a moment that Cogitator's knowledge base and inference engine could be at your disposal. Remember the anecdote of the world's scientists downloading all the world's knowledge into a computer? Assume they did that with Cogitator. What would YOUR questions be? I think my first one would be: "How can we stop the madness?"

It is society that is evil and creates evil. We are all responsible for our State of Being. The ego of the State produces all human misery. The only way to remove this evil is to identify the plutocracy and take its power away. Everything they know and intentionally hide from us can be downloaded into Cogitator, so that we do not need "leaders." They are destroying the planet with wild abandon. It is time to wake up.

"When Being is understood, Life will be recognized as neither material nor finite, but as infinite, - as God, universal good; and the belief that life, or mind, was ever in a finite form, or good in evil, will be destroyed."

From Science and Health
By Mary Baker Eddy

There are countless books for self-improvement on the shelves. Most will address what is called "success" in monetary terms. This is another illusion perpetrated by those who control the economic system. The power structure needs workers to do their bidding because it certainly doesn't know how to do anything for itself. The plutocracy must have people who are willing to believe lies in order to sustain its own illusory existence. It uses emotion to steer the course of government and ignorance to manage egos.

If you stop and examine each thought as it comes to mind, you will be able to find out the source of each and be able to make a choice as to whether or not you need it. Wisdom to me is simply the ability to change my mind. I have a favorite movie that taught me a valuable lesson. For those of you who have not seen Bill Murray in "Groundhog Day," run to anywhere you can get a copy and watch the movie. For those of you who have seen it, you may remember the story and its rather powerful message.

Bill Murray plays the role of a weatherman who has been assigned by his station to cover the Groundhog Day celebrations for Punxsutawney Phil in Punxsutawney, Pennsylvania. (If you are unaware of this yearly ritual, you can check it out at www.punxsutawneyphil.com.) It has become (like most festivals) a time for trying to break out of winter with a bit of fun. The legend is that, if Phil comes out of his burrow on February 2 and sees his shadow, it means we will have another six weeks of winter. Cute.

But, the Bill Murray character in the film does not take kindly to this assignment. He is a crusty, nasty malcontent who believes his poo-poo has no aroma. He is sent to the assignment with a beautiful co-worker and the cameraman. They get there the night before and check into their hotel for the night. When the next morning comes, the main character, (Bill Murray) is roused by the bedside radio with "Good Morning! It's Groundhog Day! The weather for today is..." He wakes up and gloomily contemplates his miserable day. You can imagine his thoughts by his demeanor. (How did I get stuck in this crap? I surely am better than this job. Why would they want to send someone of my status to this gig?) Can you just see that face?

He continues his gloomy outlook throughout his morning routine and heads to the elevators and downstairs. There, he greets the staff as he wends his way to the lobby and proceeds to go to the site of the shoot for the event. Along the way, he has several chance encounters with other characters in the movie and his sour attitude is displayed in each encounter. His obnoxious behavior continues during and after the shoot of the Groundhog Day event and he ends his day by acting obnoxious enough towards the female lead to go to bed empty and alone. He learned nothing today.

The next morning, he is awakened again by the bedside radio with the words: "Good Morning! It's Groundhog Day! The weather for today is..." At first, he has to collect his thoughts to ensure he is not dreaming and, although he finds it odd, thinks no more of it. When he finishes his morning routine and heads downstairs as he had the previous day, he encounters the same people and is confronted with the same words and conduct as the prior day. Now, he begins to wonder more about what he is experiencing. As he again proceeds towards the site of the shoot, (he doesn't know what else to do!) the events of the previous day replay themselves on his path. His behavior during the day changes ever so slightly from before and he goes back to the hotel that night paying a bit more attention to his experience. The following morning starts the very same way as the previous two and, for sure, he is now paying more attention to his day.

He is still not sure about what is happening, so he decides to try something different this day. Since he knows what the people he meets will say to him from previous experience, he prepares himself for each anticipated answer before he meets the person. He wants to see what happens if he changes his behavior and words. One day, he brings doughnuts to the shoot for the female lead and the cameraman. They are so stunned to find a considerate gesture in this person that they actually smile and thank him kindly. He is not accustomed to this kind of response from people, but he finds it rather pleasant to be liked for a change. This day ends on a slightly more favorable note, but rejection at its end still happens. He is on his way, however.

The movie flashes through countless Groundhog Days and depicts the main character trying to leave the day through all kinds of behaviors. He puts himself in all kinds of situations to change the circumstances and get out of the day. Nothing works, not even suicide. He kills himself a number of times, sometimes in ridiculous fashion, but always wakes up to Groundhog Day. He finally stops thinking of himself and begins thinking about the day. "If I'm going to be stuck in this day forever, what can I change today to make the day more pleasant?" The answer becomes obvious. He will try to take advantage of replaying the day to get his coworker to bed. So, he begins.

The following days are executed showing him paying attention to his behavior in a totally focused way. He starts with the reaction he got when he brought dough-nuts and tries to extend the feeling by modifying his behavior. Each time the magic is broken and he gets rejected, he changes the behavior from that point on in the new day. Eventually, the female lead has fallen in love with him and goes further and further towards the hotel bed as he improves his behavior. However, he continually ruins the trust in the relationship before they can consummate the relationship because he is still being selfish in his desire.

The movie ends when he finally releases his selfish-ness and truly falls in love with her. He finds love. As soon as that happens, she recognizes it and goes to bed with him. He made it through the day without selfish-ness. The last scene of the movie begins the next day with something other than: "It's Groundhog Day!" and the couple can get on with their now happy lives. Love was the answer.

This movie can be the template of your own life. If you go through each of your days making the same mis-takes as the previous day, you will have to suffer your unwillingness to learn. The mistakes will pop up again until you understand what caused them and remove the behavior that causes you pain.

If you really believed your ego dies every night and is reborn every morning and you also believed you will always wake up, you will have an eternity to create your day the way you want to see it. Start changing your behavior. It begins by analyzing your ego's mistakes. Every one of them is a potential lesson for improvement. All mistakes will cause us some pain, but, once we know what caused them, we get relief. DO NOT HIDE YOUR MISTAKES! They will surely come back if you do. Instead, try to remember your last mistake and find the element that will remove it forever. Debug yourself.

Conclusion

"I count religion as a childish toy and hold there is no sin but ignorance."

Christopher Marlowe

One of the offshoots of the Rosicrucians is the Martinist branch. The founder of this theosophy was Louis Claude de Saint-Martin, born in 1743. His philosophy was founded upon the time-honored propositions of the ancient Wisdom-Religion. He states:

"How can any order of things subsist if there were not a Substance of Life disseminated everywhere? There **must** be a living Essence behind the manifested universe, a Life-Substance which is the groundwork of existence, One Actuality which every man perceives as **himself**."

Another passage from Saint-Martin:

"Why does man suffer? Because he has identified himself with the external universe. If man would only for a moment take a more correct view of the matter, he would recognize the dignity of his being and his superiority over the external order. The lower kingdoms express the laws of nature. The animal can use those laws. But the Spirit-Man has at once the effect, the use and the free direction of those laws. The lower Mysteries deal with the laws of the physical universe, but the Higher Mysteries are concerned with man's **real** being and its relation to the Divine Principle. The final intent of the Higher Mysteries is to arouse Compassion and show man his responsibility to the lower kingdoms."

Wisdom from the East:

The Tao is described as one, but the moment it becomes manifest, it has to become two. Manifestation must be dual; it cannot be singular. It has to become matter and consciousness; it has to become man and woman, day and night, life and death. You will find these two principles everywhere. The whole of life is these two principles and behind them is hidden the One. If you continue to remain involved in these dualities, in the polar opposites, you will remain in the world. If you use your intelligence, if you become a little more alert and start looking into the depth of things, you will be surprised – the opposites are not really opposites – but complementaries. And behind them both is one single energy – that is Tao.

When we whine and revile we give power to that which we revile and whine about. We cease to be in charge of our life. I love the way that Wayne Dyer describes it in You'll See It When You Believe It. He says, "I no longer view the world in terms of unfortunate accidents or misfortunes. I know in my being that I influence it all, and now find myself considering why I created a situation, rather than saying, "why me?" This heightened awareness directs me to look inside of myself for answers. I take responsibility for all of it, and the interesting puzzle becomes a fascinating challenge when I decide to influence areas of my life in which I previously believed I was not in control. I now feel that I control it all.

It is interesting and also somewhat distressing that so much of the wisdom found hundreds of years ago (even thousands) should be so unknown in today's world. Before television, people actually had to think for themselves, I suppose. Eastern philosophy is much older than Western philosophy and seems to be gaining more exposure lately. Gautam Siddharta became a Buddha at least five hundred years before Jesus became a Christ. A Buddha and a Christ is the same thing. Both have to destroy the human ego to become divine. Gautam Siddharta sat under a bhodi tree for three years to finally be able to explain existence as a human being. I think it quite possible that Jesus read Buddhist texts before he went back to Palestine.

"If Jesus Christ were to come today, people would not even crucify him. They would ask him to dinner, hear what he had to say, and make fun of it."

Thomas Carlyle

If you can make people think what you want them to think, you have control over what they do. Human egos are very susceptible to suggestion. That is what hypnotism is about – the power of suggestion. Cultural indoctrination and imperialism is what creates schools of thought that make groups follow a certain set of rules. The plutocracy makes the rules. If you cannot control your thoughts and emotions, you are subject to these rules. Tradition, institutions and the like are examples of imitative behavior that is virtually useless in the real universe. They are habits, schools of thought, and passed on for no other reason than lack of imagination.

Traditions, superstitions and institutions need to be examined for their validity. Much of ego's activity is based upon imitation. Since ego does not want to be a pariah, it will conform to the ways of the herd and start building its ego jar early in its development. Inevitably, especially in today's Information Age, ego will feel disease about doing what "society" is imposing upon it. The beliefs and values that created the laws of the past simply do not apply in a more enlightened community.

Ego, being a very delicate structure, strengthens itself by doing comparisons to what it perceives in other egos. The bigger the group, the bigger the individual ego. All kinds of groups get created by this "need to belong" and this is the need that group egos will exploit in order to stay alive. Countless human group activities exist for the perpetration of faith, belief and values. All faiths, beliefs and values are illusory and serve the purpose of subjecting egos to "group-think." The more activities provided to ego, the less it can think for itself.

What faith, belief and value provide ego is hope. The weak egos who continually hope to win the lottery; that Jesus will return; that the end of the world is near, etc. are all hoping that some external force will come into their reality and bring them peace. This hogwash is foisted on much of the population to have them contribute to the messengers' coffers. If the message is hope, knowledge is absent.

There is no question that humans can extricate themselves from the selfish desires of ego. It is a willful decision to do so. It is time to stop trying to be happy and begin being joyful. It is time to stop thinking that the "external" world is not created by your own thoughts. The only place to start is within you. If enough people wake up to the truth of existence, things will change at amazing speed.

Cogitator can help put us on the road to a better future. It is pure folly to be destroying the planet for the sake of having toys. There is no fun anyone can have that can be better than being joyful. Amusement is waste. It is a distraction from the true bliss you can have permanently.

You do not exist to go to war, to worry about your makeup or your abs, to concern yourself about some imaginary death, or any other ego concerns. You exist to find the source of your existence. It is right here, right now, in you. The only God there is exists in YOU. You define the power and creativity He will give you. Ask and ye shall receive. We live in heaven – it's a shame that so many egos try to create hell.

Printed in the United States
74410LV00003B/154-1098